Adath
Jeshurun
CONGREGATION

עדת ישורון

לעולם ילמד אדם ממי שהוא חפץ

*A person learns from Torah from
a person s/he admires*
Midrash Yalkul Shimoni
In appreciation of your dedication to the
Adath Jeshurun Congregation's
Shabbat Morning Program

Len Rosenfield

May 13, 2006   15 Iyar 5766

Traces
of God

Other Jewish Lights Books by Neil Gillman

The Death of Death: Resurrection and Immortality in Jewish Thought

The Jewish Approach to God: A Brief Introduction for Christians

The Way Into Encountering God in Judaism

Traces
of God

Seeing God
in Torah,
History and
Everyday Life

NEIL GILLMAN

JEWISH LIGHTS Publishing
Woodstock, Vermont

Traces of God:
Seeing God in Torah, History and Everyday Life

2006 First Printing
© 2006 by Neil Gillman

For information regarding permission to reprint material from this book, please write or fax your request to Jewish Lights Publishing, Permissions Department, at the address / fax number listed below, or e-mail your request to permissions@jewishlights.com.

Library of Congress Cataloging-in-Publication Data
Gillman, Neil.
Traces of God : seeing God in Torah, history and everyday life / Neil Gillman.
p. cm.
Includes bibliographical references and index.
ISBN 1-58023-249-3
1. God (Judaism)   2. God—Biblical teaching.   3. Bible. O.T. Pentateuch—Theology.   4. Bible. O.T. Pentateuch—Criticism, interpretation, etc.   5. Spiritual life—Judaism.   I. Title.
BM610.G525 2006
296.3'114—dc22
2005035116

Manufactured in the United States of America
Jacket Design: Tim Holtz

Published by Jewish Lights Publishing
A Division of LongHill Partners, Inc.
Sunset Farm Offices, Route 4, P.O. Box 237
Woodstock, VT 05091
Tel: (802) 457-4000   Fax: (802) 457-4004
www.jewishlights.com

FOR SARAH

Contents

Introduction

TWENTY-FIVE YEARS AGO, I was invited by the administration of the Jewish Theological Seminary, the school with which I have been associated for more than fifty years, to serve as one of three regular contributors to "The Sabbath Week" column in *The Jewish Week*, New York's Anglo-Jewish weekly. I was to be the voice of the Conservative movement, joining Rabbis Shlomo Riskin and Lawrence Hoffman, who were representing the Orthodox and Reform movements respectively. I was replacing Rabbi Gerson D. Cohen, then Chancellor of the Seminary, whose illness had forced him to withdraw from this assignment.

Since then, to this day, every three weeks with absolute regularity, I submit a column on that week's Torah portion. I typically begin with the Torah reading itself, though from time to time, I use the haftarah or the themes of an upcoming festival. To my great good fortune, *The Jewish Week* has allowed me total freedom both to choose the theme and to express my opinion. I am grateful to the publisher and editors of *The Jewish Week* for this latitude and for permitting me to publish this anthology.

My field is Jewish theology, so it is not at all surprising that much of my writing deals with that subject. I have reflected on some of the pervasive issues in the field, on questions that continue to trouble me or that engage my attention in my Seminary classes, always trying to ground my thinking on the biblical text. Frequently, these brief discussions have served as a preliminary statement of conclusions that later appeared in my published books.

Shortly after being invited to write, I had a chance encounter with Larry Hoffman and asked him about his experience with the column. He replied that it was a double gift. First, he was now reviewing the Torah reading week by week; second, nothing else that he had ever written had such a wide readership as these statements. After twenty years, I can testify that he was absolutely right on both counts.

For the purposes of this anthology I have selected roughly one third of these columns. My selections were based first, on my personal judgment as to their relative merit, and second, on the extent to which theology was central to the discussion. In each selection, I have eliminated all explicit references to the Torah portion that originally prompted the reflection, but those references can be found in the "Index of Torah Readings" located at the end of the book. I have done little further editing. What you read now is more or less what I originally wrote. Also, I have ignored the original sequence in which these reflections originally appeared. Instead, I have arranged them according to four broad themes.

ABOUT THE TRANSLATION

Unless noted, the Bible translation I have used in this book is almost entirely from the Jewish Publication Society translation of the *Tanakh* (1985). This translation uses what we today recognize as masculine God language. This is in contrast to the language that I have used in my own writing throughout the book, but I leave the masculine God language intact to preserve the authenticity of the citations.

ACKNOWLEDGMENTS

This volume could never have been published without the help of two of my rabbinical students who have worked closely with me as my research assistants. Dan Ain, in particular, reviewed all of the material I had written during these twenty-five years and made a preliminary selection of those pieces that he felt were most appropriate for inclusion. Dan's mastery of the technological skills that have become indispensable in modern-day publishing was simply indispensable. Ben Kramer reviewed my final selections, prepared the index, and checked all biblical and rabbinic references for accuracy. My gratitude to both Dan and Ben is unbounded.

I write these lines as Rabbi Ismar Schorsch approaches the final months of his career as Chancellor of the Seminary. Rabbi Schorsch has been unfailingly generous with his support and encouragement of my teaching and writing throughout the decades that we have been colleagues. I use this opportunity to express my gratitude for his many kindnesses on my behalf throughout the years and to wish him well as he embarks on another phase of his accomplished career.

I work daily in a rich center of Jewish life and thought. Whatever I have accomplished as a rabbi and teacher of Judaism, I owe to the Seminary. Not a day goes by without my learning from an extraordinary group of faculty colleagues. I have also long realized that my most insightful teachers have been the generations of students that have come to study with me. They will recognize their contributions to my thinking on every page of this volume.

This is the fourth volume that I have entrusted to the publishing skills of Stuart M. Matlins, publisher of Jewish Lights, and his staff. Scholars often compare notes about their misadventures with the various publishers with whom they have had to deal. I listen to their tales of woe with astonishment. Working with Jewish Lights is a dream, largely because of Stuart and his staff, particularly Emily Wichland, who nursed this volume with the same gentle care that she has my previous books.

Nothing has meant more to me, throughout the years, than the constant love and support of my daughters, Abby and Debby, and my sons-in-law, Michael and Danny. My grandchildren, Jacob, Ellen, Livia, and Judah serve as my personal fountain of youth. They keep me young and revitalize everything I do.

I dedicate this volume to my wife, Sarah, who frequently serves as my sounding board as I prepare to write these pieces, who is usually the first person to read them as they are published, who continues to be my most perceptive critic, and who has long urged me to publish this anthology.

Finally, it is a perpetual source of radical amazement to me that as I enter my eighth decade, I continue to enjoy God's gifts of mind and heart that enable me to teach Torah. For these gifts, in the words of the liturgy, I praise God daily for having kept me in life, for sustaining me, and for enabling me to reach this moment.

PART 1

Seeing God

Connecting the Dots

"WE DIDN'T CONNECT THE DOTS."

We heard this refrain again and again as American intelligence agencies tried to explain why they failed to anticipate the attacks of September 11, 2001. They acknowledged that in retrospect, there were many pieces of evidence that an attack was forthcoming, but what analysts failed to see was how the pieces fit together. They could not discern a coherent, overall pattern. They saw the individual dots, but they were unable to connect them. That was their failure.

The analogy of connecting the dots refers to a childhood game in which we are given a page with dots. Next to every dot is a number; when we followed the sequence of numbers and connect the dots, we get a picture. The problem facing the Central Intelligence Agency was that they were faced with an infinite number of dots. Which should they notice and which should they ignore? And their dots had no numbers.

Professor Jeffery Tigay, in his Jewish Publication Society commentary to the book of Deuteronomy, writes that "chapter 4 is the theological heart of Deuteronomy." This chapter serves as Israel's guidebook on connecting the dots of their experience: what dots to connect and what dots to ignore; how to connect them and how not to connect them.

Sprinkled throughout the chapter are references to seeing. Mentioned first, what Israel did see: "You saw with your own eyes what the Lord did in the matter of Baal-Peor, that the Lord your God wiped out from among you every person who followed Baal-Peor" (Deut. 4:3). Also noted is what Israel did not see: "The Lord spoke to you out of the fire; you heard the sound of words but perceived no shape" (Deut. 4:12). The people are warned as well that they might forget what they saw: "But take utmost care and watch yourselves scrupulously, so that you do not forget the things that you saw with your own eyes" (Deut. 4:9).

The author of this text is most emphatically not a rationalist. The way to God is not through rational argumentation but rather through experience. This author is not an early Maimonides. Among contemporary theologians, he is the predecessor for Abraham Joshua Heschel and Mordecai Kaplan, both of whom, despite many differences in substance, are religious empiricists. To put it another way, this author appeals not to reason but rather to history as a record of God's presence. Inquire about bygone ages, this author suggests. Has anything as grand as this ever happened? Has any nation heard the voice of a god speaking out of a fire? Has any god ventured to go and take for himself one nation from the midst of another? Therefore, the obvious conclusion: "It has been clearly demonstrated to you that the Lord alone is God" (Deut. 4:32–35).

Among medieval thinkers, this author is the model for Yehuda Halevi. In his *Kuzari,* one of the most fascinating books ever penned by a Jewish thinker, Halevi's argument for the superiority of Judaism over Christianity and Islam rests on the record of God's relationship with Israel as narrated in Torah. Indeed, he begins his defense of Judaism by telling a story—the story of Jewish history!

Chapter 4 is the "theological heart" of Deuteronomy because biblical theology is based on experience. If we were to ask the Bible how we may gain an awareness of God's presence in the world, the answer would be, "Just look!" Look at nature. Look at your history. The Bible is a textbook on the dynamics of the religious experience.

But problems abound, as the verses above suggest. First, we have to want to look. That explains why Moses spends so much effort urging his people to look and to see.

Second, we must look at the right things—not, for example, "at the sun and the moon and the stars," for we might conclude that we are to worship them in place of God (Deut. 4:19). Then there is always the danger that we might forget what we have seen. Communal memory is very fragile.

Finally, no matter how hard we look, the God of Israel cannot be seen. Looking is not seeing, and seeing God is not like seeing an apple. It is much more like making a medical diagnosis on the basis of looking at a complex set of symptoms. Each of the symptoms is a dot. We can look at each of the dots and still miss the pattern. Making a diagnosis requires us to decide which symptoms to ignore, which to include, and how to fit together those that we do include so that they form a coherent pattern. It's a matter of connecting the dots.

In this way, religious education is very much like medical education. Both involve teaching students how to connect the dots, how to see complex patterns and decide what these patterns mean. The major difference between the two is that with respect to medical education, the scope of the evidence is rather narrow. In religious education, in contrast, the scope is the broadest possible canvas: all of nature and history, the gamut of human experience, taken together to form one complex whole.

The Torah is replete with references to hearing God but contains precious few references to seeing God. What we look for and see are traces of God's presence in the world and in history, but not God. Seeing is very complicated. For those traces to become identified as reflections of God's presence requires a good deal of interpretation. That is precisely what this text tries to accomplish.

In short, contrary to the popular adage, seeing is not believing. Rather, we see what we already believe, what we are conditioned or educated to see, what we expect to see. Seeing is not at all the passive activity we commonly understand it to be. We bring a good deal of ourselves into everything we see. As my ophthalmologist constantly reminds me, we don't see with our eyes, we see with our brain.

Despite what we may believe, seeing is an incredibly subjective experience. People often disagree vigorously about what they see. This is why Moses goes into such detail, not only by instructing the Israelites regarding what they should and should not see, but, more important, by giving the interpretation, that is, in the brainwork regarding what their eyes have seen. To my mind, then, the whole task of Jewish religious education is to train another generation of Jews in how to see, what to see, and how to interpret what they see as religious Jews. For this task, our primary textbook is the Bible and chapters such as this one.

Faith in a Silent God

WOULDN'T WE ALL WANT TO have a decisive, irrefutable proof that God exists?

The extraordinary narrative found in I Kings 18:1–39, which serves as the haftarah on those weeks when we recite the story of the Golden Calf, claims to provide such a proof. Despite its form, it is among the most striking theological statements in scripture. At the center of the story stands that enigmatic early prophet, Elijah, who challenges the Israelites: "How long will you keep hopping between two opinions? If the Lord is God, follow God; and if Baal, follow him!" (I Kings 18:21).

Elijah then designs a decisive test that will demonstrate forever and for everyone which is really God. The prophets of Baal choose a bull and prepare it for sacrifice. Elijah asks them to invoke Baal to send a fire that will consume their sacrifice. They pray "from morning until noon" (I Kings 18:26), but nothing happens. Elijah mocks them: "Shout louder! ... Perhaps he is asleep and will wake up" (I Kings 18:27). They continue through the afternoon, they gash themselves, but still nothing.

Then Elijah gathers the Israelites, builds an altar, pours water over the sacrificial bull three times, and prays, "Answer me, O Lord, answer me, that this people may know that You, O Lord, are God." Fire descends from heaven and consumes everything, whereupon the people fling themselves on their faces and cry out, "The Lord alone is God! The Lord alone is God!"

I wish that God would appear to me as irrefutably as God appeared to Elijah. Of course, I quickly remind myself, first, that I am not Elijah; second, that maybe God does appear to me in a decisive way but I don't see it; and finally, that the whole story is told from the biblical perspective, which assumes God does create miracles and it will turn out right at the end.

This story of Elijah at Mount Carmel has entered the literature of philosophy of religion as the paradigm of the kind of proof for God's existence that turns some into believers and leaves others unconvinced. But the most disturbing question addressed to this story is posed by the eminent Jewish theologian-philosopher Emil Fackenheim. He asks: What would Elijah have done if God had not answered his call? if a fire had descended to consume the sacrifice to Baal?

One thing is clear, Fackenheim answers: Elijah would not have converted to the worship of Baal. He would have continued to work for God, even in the face of God's silence or absence. For Elijah, then, the test was not a test; he did not need to verify his faith. Evidence for God did not lead him to believe in the first place, and contrary evidence would not have turned him into an atheist or a Baal worshiper. Elijah's faith was not based on experience. The evidence, pro or con, was irrelevant.

To use a contemporary label, Elijah was an existentialist. His faith was an act of absolute trust, a "leap" into the unknown, not subject to proof or disproof. As for the people? They seem to have been convinced for the moment. But as we know, they quickly forgot, or ignored, or denied what their eyes had seen and returned to idolatry. Was this Elijah's "failure"? Probably not, for I doubt whether a miracle of comparable magnitude would be any more effective today. God is simply not subject to "scientific" proofs of this kind. We are inherently skeptical of the miraculous. We have been weaned on the scientific temper that demands a different quality of proof before we commit ourselves to a truth.

Still, Fackenheim's question haunts me. Our God so frequently does not respond to our call. Our God does not appear on demand. We are more struck by God's absence in times of acute trauma. The Bible knows of those moments as well; witness Job, for example, or Psalms 13 and 44. Our experience leads us to feel that belief in God is not demonstrable.

What does matter is where we choose to cast our lot. Our choice is not God or Baal, but God or one of the many idols such as fame, wealth, or our nation, or substitute gods that we use to lend coherence to our lives.

Finally, we cannot ignore the liturgical echoes of the concluding words of the story. To this day we conclude the Yom Kippur service by repeating "The Lord alone is God." The Israelites on Mount Carmel repeated it twice. We repeat it seven times, possibly because we do not have the overwhelming evidence which that community had just experienced. Or possibly because in the light of modern history, we have to reassure ourselves.

Perceiving God's Presence

H OW DO WE KNOW FOR SURE when God is present?
In describing Abraham's encounter with God, the Torah states that the "Lord appeared to him by the trees of Mamre; he was sitting at the entrance of the tent as the day grew hot. Looking up, he saw three men standing near to him" (Gen. 18:1–2). These two brief verses are rich in theological possibilities. According to this text, it was God who appeared to Abraham. But what did Abraham actually see? Three men.

One can ask: What else was Abraham supposed to see? The biblical God usually does not appear in physical form. When we talk about perceiving the presence of God, we typically mean a kind of perception that is not purely sensory. What we literally see is a natural event, such as a magnificent sunset, or an extraordinary historical event, such as the creation of the State of Israel. But we then interpret what we see as manifesting God's presence in nature and history.

Yet what gives us the right to make that interpretation? And how do we know for sure that the interpretation is right? And what do we do with all of those other experiences of God that we dismiss as manifestly illusory or hallucinatory? How do we distinguish between the two?

My attention was drawn to this text by a letter written in 1924 by the German Jewish philosopher Franz Rosenzweig to his colleagues at the Frankfurt Lehrhaus, the Jewish education program created by Rosenzweig and his colleague Martin Buber. The letter, published in *On Jewish Learning*, edited by Rosenzweig's student Nahum N. Glatzer, forms the climax of an extended correspondence between Rosenzweig and Buber on the subject of revelation and law.

The main issue under discussion in this correspondence is the relationship between the mitzvot that we are commanded to observe and God's revelation. Can we assume that all of the details of Jewish law are explicitly revealed? If we don't accept the notion that God spoke at Sinai, how do we justify what we feel we must observe and what we feel we are not obligated to observe?

Rosenzweig's position on this issue is sharply individualistic. Only the individual Jew has the right to testify that he or she is commanded by God to do a particular mitzvah. Only then is he or she obligated to perform that mitzvah. And only then can the individual precede the doing of the commandment with the blessing that articulates that God has commanded us to do whatever it is he or she is now prepared to do. No outsider can make that judgment or utter that blessing, for there are no valid objective criteria that apply in this highly personal situation. This sharp individualism is what makes Rosenzweig so appealing to our contemporaries.

But throughout the correspondence, Rosenzweig draws an analogy between the experience of being commanded and the experience of God's presence. The latter, too, is a highly personal experience, Rosenzweig insists. "As far as you [Buber] have made the experience that the Law is not God's Law ... that is a valid one, as valid as an atheism based on an experience that God does not exist." He continues: "Nor can I imagine the divine nature of the whole ... in any other sense than that of Rabbi Nobel's powerful five-minute sermon on God's appearing below Abraham's tent: 'And God appeared to Abraham ... and he lifted his eyes ... and behold: three men.'" (Rabbi Nehemiah Nobel was a prominent German rabbi who had exerted a decisive influence on Rosenzweig's return to Judaism a decade earlier.)

The analogy is between the individualism that shapes Rosenzweig's notion of being commanded and that which shapes our recognition of God. Abraham, in a literal sense, "saw" three men. But Abraham, out of his own, personal experience, testified that what he saw was God. And that perception was absolutely true for Abraham.

The message of our text and of Rosenzweig's interpretation on it suggests that ultimately the determination that God is present to us is a highly personal and individual experience. Of course, we have to be sensitized to perceive the presence of God—that is the entire purpose of the rituals and liturgies of religion. We also need a vocabulary to help us identify what we experience, and that is the goal of Jewish religious education. Finally, at least in Judaism, we need a community, for ultimately it is our religious community, through its centuries of shared experience, that sensitizes us and gives us the vocabulary to guide, shape, and structure our multiple individual experiences.

Still, in the last analysis, with all of these structures in place, there is never any objective guarantee that what we experience is God. At this point, personal testimony takes over. The atheist who testifies to his personal experience that no God is present has to be taken seriously. So do those who claim that God is palpably present when, for example, we light candles Friday night, or give birth to a child, or watch a magnificent sunrise, or walk through Jerusalem on Shabbat, or stand under the chuppah.

Surely, then, this answers one of the burning questions raised by the terrifying story that concludes our Torah reading, the story of the *Akedah*, or binding of Isaac. How did Abraham know that it was God who commanded him to bring his son as a sacrifice? How did he know that it was not an illusion, or even Satan?

The only possible answer is that Abraham *knew*, just as he knew that it was not three men but really God who appeared to him on that hot day in Mamre. His personal experience was absolutely decisive. There was no objective criterion that led him to that decision, nor could there be. At the end, one sees what one sees, one experiences what one experiences—and one testifies to that experience with one's entire life.

God's When and Where

WHEN MY GRANDDAUGHTER WAS FIVE YEARS OLD, she was already a budding theologian. During a visit, she delivered a spontaneous lecture on the question "Where is God?" Her answer, of course: "God is everywhere!"

That question is quite familiar to her grandfather. My standard answer is that obviously God is not in a place, not in space, neither above (in the heavens) nor below, neither outside nor, as many suggest, inside me, "in my heart." The "where" question simply does not apply to God. Here I echo the midrashic notion that God is the place of the world, not the other way around. That's why one of the names for God is *HaMakom*, literally "The Place."

A colleague of mine, Professor Steven Brown, has suggested that rather than asking "Where is God?" we should ask "When is God?" Rather than looking for God in space, we should look for God in time, at sanctified moments, not in sanctified places. There are moments when God seems to be more accessible to us than others, and those moments provide a clue to understanding what God means to us.

But whether in space or in time, what does it mean to say that God is "accessible"? What do we experience when we experience God's presence? Is this experience a seeing? But then, what precisely do we see? How do we see the unseeable?

In my teaching, I am regularly confronted by these questions and the confusing biblical reports of God appearing to human beings. We know that on one occasion, Moses was told that he cannot see God's face but only God's back (Ex. 33:23). But after Moses dies, he is referred to as having been singled out by God "face to face" (Deut. 34:10). So which is it?

God appears to Abraham, but when Abraham looks up, all he sees is "three men" (Gen. 18:2). In the Prophets, Isaiah does behold "my Lord seated on a high and lofty throne" (Is. 6:1); that's surely an answer to the "where" question. But Ezekiel sees something much more elusive, "the appearance of the semblance of the Presence of the Lord" (Ez. 1:28).

Then we have the totally mystifying passage where Moses, Aaron, Nadab, Abihu, and seventy elders ascend the mountain, apparently an answer to the "where" question. "They saw the God of Israel. Under God's feet there was the likeness of a pavement of sapphire, like the very sky for purity. Yet God did not raise God's hand against the leaders of the Israelites; they beheld God, and they ate and drank" (Ex. 24:9–11).

What is striking about this passage is the utter naturalness of the whole episode. It is "the God of Israel" that they see, not Ezekiel's "appearance of the semblance of the Presence of the Lord." But they are not harmed, possibly a reference to Exodus 33:20, where Moses is told that no human can see God and live. Then they eat and drink! Hardly the reaction we would expect from human beings who are seeing God. And God has feet?

In this passage, both the "where" and the "when" questions seem to be appropriate. God is beheld on the mountain, a reference to the site of the revelation of Torah a few verses earlier. Many people have an experience of God in nature, at sunsets or sunrises, or in a rainbow, or in the drama of a storm.

But the "when" question is also appropriate here. This scene occurs during the Torah portion *Mishpatim*, which contains the first extensive legal code in the Bible. This legal code is embedded in a narrative that begins with the redemption from slavery and reaches its climax in God's revelation of Torah and the sealing of the covenant with Israel. The last verses of this parashah describe the ritual ratification of the covenant. Exodus/Sinai, then, is one single experience, the transformatory experience that created Judaism and the Jewish people. It is at the climax of this experience that the elders have their vision of God. This would be their answer to the question "When is God?"

I do not share my granddaughter's certainty that God is everywhere. I certainly have never seen God as Isaiah, Moses, or the elders did. I'm not even sure that I have even shared Ezekiel's "appearance of the semblance of the Presence of the Lord." If anything, I'm closer to Abraham, who saw three men when it was God all the time. But I have experienced those rare unaccountable moments that in retrospect were as revelatory for me as the elders' experience was for them.

I suspect that many of us have had such moments, possibly because in our own rough and ready way, we too are prepared by our own life experience to see beyond what is immediately present to us. We will never see what those elders saw in the course of their history, and we will surely never see God as they did. But we may have our own experiences of God's presence in our lives, which may be as transformatory as theirs was.

God, Hidden and
Revealed

O N THE FACE OF IT, the fact that the Torah portion *Mikketz* is
always read on Shabbat Chanukah is pure coincidence. The
Torah reading cycle was not coordinated with the cycle of festivals and special days in our liturgical calendar, which is why we
must look to the independently designated Festival Torah, or
maftir readings, and to the *haftarot* for echoes of the appropriate
festival themes. Nevertheless, the two narratives of Joseph in
Egypt and of the Maccabean struggle against their Hellenistic
oppressors bear a closer comparison.

First the Joseph story. This gripping narrative was composed
and can be read on purely naturalist terms. It is gripping specifically because it portrays people behaving in thoroughly natural
ways toward other people. It is a story of sibling rivalry, parental
meddling, deception, lust, political ambition, guilt, and revenge.
We know these feelings. We see them in operation in our own
lives, and we can identify with the characters of the story as they
act out their roles.

What is striking about this narrative as it plays itself out is the way in which God's hand is kept thoroughly behind the scenes. Only in a few episodes, when Joseph interprets dreams (Gen. 40:8 and 41:25), particularly when he reveals his true identity to his brothers (Gen. 45:4–5), and again later after Jacob's death (Gen. 50:20), is God identified as the One who has guided the events of the story: "[Al]though you intended me harm, God intended it for good, so as to bring about the present result—the survival of many people," Joseph says to his guilt-ridden brothers.

Compare this narrative with the story of the Exodus from Egypt. Here, God is present front and center in very demonstrative ways. God speaks; the bush burns but is not consumed; plagues are delivered; miracles are performed; the sea is split; God descends on a mountaintop amid dense clouds, thunder and lightning, and the sound of the shofar. In the Joseph story, God's presence is well hidden. Here, God never speaks but is portrayed as working all along, though in ways that are not discernible to most of the participants.

The events we celebrate on Chanukah are not to be found in the Bible. To learn of them, we have to turn to extrabiblical texts such as the apocryphal books of the Maccabees, to the histories of Josephus, or to other historical sources of the period.

I first studied the history of the Maccabean revolt from scholarly histories written by professors of ancient Jewish history, and from the lectures of my teacher, the late Gerson Cohen. To my amazement, the story as they told it had little to do with the story told annually in my childhood synagogue school. The main difference between the two versions is that in the version I learned in my youth, it was God who directed the entire story. In the scholarly histories, God was singularly absent.

It was our ancestors who put God into the Chanukah story. Like the Joseph story, it can be told in thoroughly natural ways, as the story of an oppressed people rebelling against an imperialistic kingdom, fighting to regain their freedom and their right to worship as they wished, and winning because of their superior military and political sagacity. That it was God who miraculously enabled them to triumph is a matter of historical interpretation, not history.

Our ancestors saw miracles in that story, but since the miraculous dimension is not self-evident, they differed on precisely what the miracle was. In the Al Hanissim liturgy that we recite numerous times during the eight days, the miracle is the military victory of the weak over the strong, the few over the many, the pure over the impure, and the righteous over the wicked. In the Hanerot Hallalu recited over the candles, it is even more vaguely the salvation and the battles God performed for our ancestors. Only in the Talmudic version (*Shabbat* 21b) is there mention of the single cruse of oil that miraculously burned for eight days.

At the other extreme, scholars of ancient religions such as the late Theodor Gaster suggest that the origins of Chanukah lie in none of the above, but rather in the ancient pagan practice of lighting fires at the winter solstice in order to reawaken the dying sun. That's the "real" reason why we light the candles ascending from one to eight as *Beit Hillel* ordains, rather than descending from eight to one, as *Beit Shammai* would have it.

God does not appear to us in burning bushes, splitting seas, thunder and lightning, and shofar calls. But that does not mean that God is not present to us, in "the miracles that are with us daily" as the Amidah would have it, if we but put God into the stories of our lives and our times.

Because our ancestors put God into the Chanukah story, we now recite blessings that praise God for having commanded us to light the Chanukah candles, though, of course, God never did any such thing. We may be able to regain a measure of that liturgical creativity if we too can learn to see God's presence in the patterns of nature and history as they did.

Discerning the Hand of God

MY ANNUAL ENCOUNTER WITH THE STORY of Isaac's blessing of Jacob, instead of Esau, inevitably reignites a tension between two dimensions of my being: my humanist self and my religious-theological self.

My humanism sees a story of blindness and deception. Isaac is the least fully developed of the patriarchs, overshadowed by his monumental father and his complex son. Indeed, the two most significant events in Isaac's life portray him in relationships, first with his father (the *Akedah*) and then with his sons (the story of the blessing). His portrayal lacks sharp individuality.

Isaac is a transitional figure. His blindness is as much metaphorical as it is physical; he is clearly aware that it is not Esau who stands before him to receive the blessing, but in this humanist reading of the story, he is unwilling or unable to challenge his son or his wife. He is blind to the reality that failure to deal with conflict simply perpetuates it, never resolves it.

Rebecca is portrayed as strong willed, determined, and insightful. She knows her sons and her husband. She realizes that she must protect Isaac against himself, and her favorite son against his brother. She will do whatever she needs to do to accomplish her purposes.

Jacob is the deceiver; that is his name and that is his role. The message of the story is that deception breeds deception. Jacob deceives his father and is later to suffer at the hands of people who deceive him—his uncle Laban, his sons, and even his favorite son, Joseph, who was destined to spend many years in Egypt without once trying to communicate with his father.

In this reading, Esau emerges as the tragic figure. His "wild and bitter sobbing" (Gen. 27:34) on hearing of Jacob's treachery is one of the most powerful emotional outbursts in the biblical narrative. His rage is palpable, and it leads his mother to order Jacob to flee his home.

In short, this reading of the story is marked by inept parenting, family discord, intrapsychic conflict, sibling rivalry, and questionable moral behavior. But then my religious-theological side asserts itself. Here, I understand that the story is carefully fashioned to reveal the underlying thrust of biblical historiography. For we know that the entire drama is guided by the hidden hand of God.

That is why the order of covenantal succession in these Genesis narratives never follows the course of nature. It is never the firstborn who inherits God's promises, but some other son: Isaac over Ishmael, Jacob over Esau, Judah and Joseph over Reuben, Ephraim over Manasseh. This is the biblical historiographer's way of telling us that ultimately it is God who governs the course of historical events, not the immutable laws of natural order.

That is why the narrative refrains from passing any overt judgment on the behavior of these biblical personalities. It does not judge them because it knows they are acting out roles that are predetermined by a scenario that surpasses their own understanding and motivations.

Joseph spells out this message when his brothers beg his forgiveness for the way they treated him: "Am I a substitute for God? Besides, although you intended me harm, God intended it for good, so as to bring about the present result—the survival of many people" (Gen. 50:19–20). It is important for us to be reminded of that message because many of us read not only this text, but also our own historical experience from a humanist perspective. But if God is not present in history, then where is God to be found?

I struggle to reconcile these two divergent perspectives with varied results. I remain a religious humanist; my teacher was Mordecai Kaplan. I then must live with the ensuing tension, convinced that with all of the problems this creates, I am the richer for it. What also remains is my ongoing fascination with these stories, with the richness of their character development, the candor of their portrayals, their unerring insight into human behavior, and the ongoing power of their religious message.

The Value of Atheism

WE KNOW ALL TOO WELL that great piety can produce great evil. That sin can become the source of sanctification is not so obvious, however. Yet this seems to be one of the lessons in the biblical account of Korach's rebellion against Moses and Aaron.

Moses' response to Korach's challenge is to ask that each of the rebels take a fire pan with incense on it and assemble before the Lord at the entrance to the Tent of Meeting. A fire comes forth from the Lord and consumes the rebels. The Lord then instructs Moses (Num. 17:3) that Elazar the son of Aaron collect the charred fire pans from the remains of the fire, and hammer them into plating for the altar as an *ot*,—a sign, symbol, reminder, or warning—to the people of Israel. Elazar does just that. From then on, whenever the Israelites look at the altar, they will see the plating from the fire pans and recall Korach and his rebellion.

The text explains that the reason the remains of the fire pans could not simply be discarded was that they had been used for an offering to the Lord and thus had become sanctified. However unauthorized or rebellious that offering had been, it remained an offering to God. Whatever was used in the course of that worship had acquired sanctity and could not be cast aside.

On a superficial level, the point is clear. The memory of Korach's rebellion must be kept alive. The Israelites need to be reminded again and again of the disastrous results of rebellion. Hence, the plating on the altar. But a more profound interpretation of this text is suggested by Rabbi Abraham Isaac Kook as cited in a comment on Numbers 17:2–3, noted in *Etz Hayim* (2001). Atheism, Rav Kook claims, is necessary because it stands as a perpetual reminder to the community of believers, a rebuke to the inevitable corruption that accumulates around faith and religion: the tendency to anthropomorphize; to conceive of God in narrow and unrefined ways; to concentrate on the words and letters of Torah instead of on the thoughts and feelings that it expresses, and on its ultimate moral thrust. In fact, atheism's denial of the "existence" of God is totally on target, for to Rav Kook, the claim that God "exists" falls into idolatry. A stone can be said to exist. God, however, does not exist; God is beyond or above existence, the ultimate source of existence. Atheism, Rav Kook insists, is an instrument for repentance. It is also, thus, a necessary prelude to redemption.

The plating on the altar, then, is not simply a reminder of Korach's sin. It is even more a reminder of the sin that lurks in the heart of the pious, within all of us, a perpetual warning that it is not at all clear who is the saint and who is the sinner, that each of us is both saint and sinner, and the line separating the two is very murky indeed.

This is a perennial theme in the writings of my favorite "religious" novelist, Graham Greene. Greene, a Roman Catholic, delighted in portraying the ambiguities that lie in the human heart. A central figure in many of his novels is the sinner-saint— the priest in *The Power and the Glory,* or Scobie in *The Heart of the Matter,* as powerful a religious novel as was ever written. Scobie, also a Roman Catholic, is caught by war in a small backwater town in West Africa where he serves as assistant police commissioner. He drifts into an adulterous affair, but it is the ultimate integrity of the man and what the author calls his "love of God" that leads to his doom. In the end, Scobie emerges as infinitely more saintly and more of a "believer" than the official representatives of his religious community.

A strikingly contemporaneous elaboration of this theme is in Rabbi Irving "Yitz" Greenberg's contribution to *Auschwitz: Beginning of a New Era?* edited by Eva Fleischner. Greenberg suggests here that neither the simple reaffirmation of God nor the radical denial of God can stand as a legitimate theological response to the Holocaust. He draws on Martin Buber's notion of "moment gods"—that God is God only at the moment of our awareness of God's presence. For Greenberg, after Auschwitz, we must speak also of "moment faiths." "This ends the easy dichotomy of atheist/theist," Greenberg claims. "Faith is a life response of the whole person to the Presence in life and history. Like life, the response ebbs and flows. The difference between the skeptic and the believer is frequency of faith and not certitude of position."

Most important, "The rejection of the unbeliever by the believer is literally the denial or attempted suppression of what is within oneself." The tension between atheism and affirmation remains within each of us at all times. Religious faith at its most authentic is precisely the dialectic between these two poles. Faith is never something we "have" totally and thoroughly at all times. We are all, rather, perpetually in process, on the move, between the polarities of affirmation and denial.

The reason for plating the altar with the pans of the rebels is to remind us of the rebelliousness that is legitimately within ourselves. For it is never clear who is the authentic believer and who is the atheist; there is both believer and atheist within each of us. Even more, the life of faith at its most authentic necessarily includes both moments of belief and unbelief.

The Mystery of the Red Cow

WHAT IS THE PLACE OF MYSTERY IN RELIGION? The ritual of the *para aduma*, the red cow (Num. 19), is the locus classicus for the Jewish understanding of this issue. The red cow is to be totally consumed, its ashes combined with water and other substances; this new mixture then becomes the source of purification for someone who has become ritually impure by, for example, coming into contact with a corpse.

The mysterious nature of this ritual is alluded to in Rashi's opening comment to this chapter, which quotes the midrash on the term *chukat*, usually translated as "decree" (or by the Jewish Publication Society as "ritual law"). Rashi notes: "The Satan or the nations of the world taunt Israel, saying, 'What is this law all about and what is its rationale?' The Torah therefore calls it a *chukah*; it is God's decree and we must not question it."

Why do Satan and the nations of the world taunt Israel precisely about the red cow? Because although the ashes of the cow are used to purify the ritually impure, the very person who prepares this mixture of ashes and water thereby becomes ritually impure and must himself undergo the process of ritual purification.

The paradox of the red cow, then, is that it purifies the impure and defiles the pure. A more extended discussion of this paradox is discussed in a midrashic anecdote that relates how a heathen confronts Rabban Yochanan ben Zakkai with the same puzzle. Rabban Yochanan gives the heathen an apparently satisfactory and rational explanation, but the rabbi's students protest. "You deflected that heathen with a reed, but what would you say to us?" To them, he answers: "The corpse does not have the power to defile, nor does the mixture of ashes and water have the power to cleanse. The Holy One has said: 'I have set it down as a statute [*chukah*], I have issued a decree [*gezerah*]. You are not permitted to transgress it" (*Pesikta d'Rav Kahanah* 4:7).

The ArtScroll Chumash on this passage comments: "The underlying message ... is that the Supreme Intelligence has granted man a huge treasury of spiritual and intellectual gifts, but none is more precious than the knowledge that God is infinite, both in existence and in wisdom, while man is as limited in his ability to comprehend as he is in his physical existence."

But Rabbi Jacob Milgrom, in his Jewish Publication Society commentary to Numbers, insists that he can "unlock the paradox of the red cow" and proceeds to do just that in an extended excursus to this passage, based on his understanding of biblical sacrificial ritual and its relationship to ancient Near Eastern religious practices.

This tension between the mysterious or paradoxical and the intelligible or rational dimensions of religion hounds all of us, and we each must find our own resolution of that tension. My own resolution has usually tended in favor of the rational and the intelligible, probably because of my particular temperament, and because however mysterious some of the provisions of the

Torah may seem to us today, my conviction is that they must have made perfect sense to the community who first formulated them. The primary impulse behind much of contemporary Jewish scholarship is precisely to try to unearth those original meanings and thereby make sense of these institutions.

My impulse, then, is to try to understand religion in general and Judaism in particular, but I know that for other Jews, that would constitute the source of my personal heresy. An Orthodox rabbi I highly respect once responded to a lecture I gave on revelation in the Bible by saying, "Your problem is that you want to understand revelation. I don't need to understand it. I am perfectly content with believing that at a certain moment in history, God descended on a mountaintop and spoke to my ancestors. How that took place is a mystery, but I'm perfectly prepared to accept it as a mystery and to go on from there."

But I must confess I am not entirely free of hesitation, doubt, or even a measure of guilt about pursuing that quest for understanding. The reason for this is another conviction that lies at the very heart of my personal theology, namely, that God is very much beyond intelligibility by human beings.

The paradox returns then on another level. God is a mystery, beyond my understanding, yet everywhere I turn in my life as a Jew I find myself saying a great deal about this God, describing God and God's activity on earth. Were I to remain totally true to my theological convictions, I would fall silent in the face of God's overwhelming and inherently mysterious nature. But then I would be completely bereft. So I talk of God and think of God, knowing all the while that nothing my mind or my language can possibly come up with even begins to approach an adequate comprehension of God's essence.

I am totally convinced that Milgrom's very sensible understanding of the ritual of the red cow is absolutely true. But this simply deflects the dimension of the mysterious to other levels—to what Heschel calls "the startling fact that there are facts at all:

being, the universe, the unfolding of time"—and to the ultimate mystery of the One who is the source of all things and lends all things their singular integrity. In the face of this God, again to quote Heschel, "We apprehend but cannot comprehend."

Holy Tension

Τ HE MOST DIFFICULT ASPECT OF GOD'S REDEMPTION of our
ancestors from slavery in Egypt may well have been God's
attempt to persuade Moses to take on the responsibility for leading his people into freedom. The biblical narrative, usually so
teasingly spare in its details, devotes the better part of two full
chapters to the extended argument between God and Moses in
which God persuades, cajoles, and commands while Moses
resists, protests, and rejects.

The argument begins with God's appearance in the burning
bush and ends when God, in anger, assigns Aaron, Moses'
brother, to serve as Moses' mouthpiece. Note that at the end,
Moses never really says yes, he will go to Egypt. We are told simply that he returns to his father-in-law, Jethro, and informs him,
"Let me go back to my kinsmen in Egypt and see how they are
faring" (Ex. 4:18)—hardly an accurate version of what he has
been sent to do. But possibly this was as much as he was prepared to do at this point.

This tension that marks the beginning of Moses' relationship with God will continue to the very end. Moses now assumes center stage in the biblical narrative, and there is hardly a single page in that entire narrative where God and Moses are not at odds about something. Appropriately, though the biblical version of Moses' death is free of tension, the rabbinic midrash takes up this persistent theme and portrays Moses as accepting death only after a long and protracted argument with God.

Two dimensions to this tension are worth noting. The first deals with the nature of prophecy itself, the second with our personal relationship with God today.

It is extremely difficult for us today to enter into the mind-set of the biblical prophet. At a certain point in our collective history, a group of men emerged claiming to convey God's message to our ancestors. It is easy to dismiss this claim as delusional—the fruit of mental illness—or simple chicanery. Yet as Heschel points out in his monumental *The Prophets,* a phenomenological study of prophecy, part of the prophetic experience was loneliness and misery. The prophet is rarely at ease in his role.

Moses certainly felt that loneliness and misery. So did Jeremiah, who curses the day he was born, who is furious that he was not killed in his mother's womb but instead has to spend his days in toil, sorrow, and shame. Jeremiah struggles to escape his calling, to no avail. "You enticed me, O Lord, and I was enticed; You overpowered me and You prevailed. I have become a constant laughingstock, everyone jeers at me.... I thought, 'I will not mention God, no more will I speak in God's name'—but [His word] was like a raging fire in my heart ... I could not hold it in, I was helpless" (Jer. 20:7–9).

To be a prophet, then, was to live in a constant state of tension, both with the community and with God. But that tension is also inherent in the very act of faith itself for any believer. We are tempted to think of religious faith as a sinecure, as a source of calm and peacefulness. One of the best-selling books of a previous generation promised the believer "peace of mind." Nothing is further from the truth.

Any authentic believer knows full well that faith in God is a constant struggle. We never simply "have faith." Faith is not a secure possession, something we retain and hold on to as an integrated part of ourselves throughout our lifetimes. Rather, we struggle to achieve it, we lose it, regain it, lose it again, regain it again—the process is unending. A piece of us feels very much like Moses and Jeremiah. We feel overwhelmed by God who is, again to use Heschel's term, "in search" of us, who gives us no rest. Yet another piece of us resists. At other times, we are painfully aware of God's apparent absence when we ourselves are most "in search" of meaning in the face of life's absurdities. To live a life of faith is to live in constant tension.

Therefore, all of Jewish religious education must emphasize that to be an authentic believing Jew means to live in a state of perpetual ambiguity in relation to God. I mean Jewish *religious* education, not simply Jewish education. The latter is easy, a matter of teaching skills and data that all of us know how to do reasonably well. The former is infinitely more difficult, and part of the difficulty lies in the fact that a piece of us wants to make religion attractive and comforting to young people, whereas our own struggles with our personal religious commitments tells us it is rarely thus.

In this context, Moses' own struggle with God in these chapters of the Torah provides us with a valuable resource. We can neither read nor teach these exchanges without a sense of how difficult it was, even for a Moses, to accept God's call. And if it was so for Moses, who had the experience of the burning bush, how much more so for us who have little as dramatic and forceful as that experience to support our own convictions!

Abraham's Faith and Doubt

THE BIBLE IS QUITE RETICENT ABOUT DESCRIBING the qualities of its personalities. Its style is more to portray these men and women in action and then to allow us to derive their qualities from their behavior. That's why we should sit up and take notice when the Torah reports that Abraham "put his trust in the Lord and He reckoned it to his merit" (Gen. 15:6). Abraham trusted in God. The same description of Abraham appears in Nehemiah 9:8, a passage that is incorporated into our daily Shacharit (morning) service. The Jewish Publication Society translation reads, "Finding his [Abraham's] heart true to You [God]." The Hebrew root is identical in these two texts, and it is usually translated as "trust" or "loyalty."

Parenthetically, the haftarah for this Torah portion provides its own characterization of Abraham. Isaiah 41:8 refers to Abraham as "Abraham, My [God's] friend," or, more literally, "Abraham whom I love." Trust and love go together. Love demands trust, and trust implies love. Abraham's unique virtue was trust, loyalty to God.

But the dynamics of loyalty are not that simple. The paradox is that trust is not self-evident. It must be tested. We never know who our trustworthy friends are until we have called on them to act on our behalf. Until we test their loyalty, we have no right to assume it's there. The rabbinic midrash recognizes this paradox and teaches that Abraham's loyalty to God was tested ten times. The first was when God commanded him to leave his home and journey to the Holy Land. The last was when God commanded him to sacrifice his beloved son. To neither of these commands did Abraham offer a word of protest. He trusted God and he obeyed.

But Genesis 15 discloses a slightly different Abraham. One verse after commending Abraham for putting his trust in God, God promises Abraham the Holy Land as his possession. Whereupon Abraham responds, "O Lord, God, how shall I know that I am to possess it?" (Gen. 15:6–8). Where is Abraham's trust now? He seems to be saying, "OK, prove it to me!" So God grants him a vision and a covenant, formalizing God's promise.

Recall, also, that on two occasions—in Egypt in Genesis 12, and with Avimelech in Genesis 20—Abraham asks his wife, Sarah, to pass herself off as his sister lest he be killed. Where was Abraham's trust then? And when God first promises Abraham that Sarah will give him a son, we are told that "Abraham threw himself on his face and laughed, as he said to himself, 'Can a child be born to a man one hundred years old, or can Sarah bear a child at ninety?'" (Gen. 17:17). Abraham laughed, and we can assume from his private thoughts that his laughter was permeated with bitterness and despair. Where was his trust?

This portrait of Abraham, wavering between loyalty to God and doubt, goes a long way toward humanizing this paradigmatic biblical hero. He was, after all, not that different than we are. He trusted God, but his trust was also permeated with moments of profound doubt. Such a portrait speaks volumes for us. Many of us struggle with the notion that we are supposed to have "faith in God." Faith, in this context, is ambiguous, but in Judaism it is much closer to trust than to the conventional synonym, "belief."

Belief is too intellectual; trust is existential. It is an act not of the mind but of the whole person—mind, emotion, will, and behavior, taken all together. It is more a matter of "believing in" than "believing that." To "believe in" someone—our surgeon, for example—is to trust that person.

We expect that this state of faith is something that some of us attain and then hold on to for the rest of our lives. Abraham teaches us that this is not the case. There is no faith that is not riddled with doubt, and no doubt that is not marked by moments of faith.

Faith and doubt exist in a dynamic relationship, and we too, like Abraham, move back and forth between these polarities. The most helpful point of all of this is that our moments of disbelief are not to be dismissed. They are an intrinsic and valuable moment in our journey to faith in God.

Looking and Seeing

T HE UNIFYING MOTIF FOR THE TORAH PORTION *Sh'lach Lecha* is looking and seeing. The giveaway is a Hebrew word that appears in two very different contexts: once at the very beginning of the portion, in its second verse (Num. 13:2), and again at its very end, in its third to last verse (Num. 15:39). That Hebrew word is *tur*.

At the outset, the context is Moses' instructions to the twelve men he sends to reconnoiter the land of Canaan. At the end, the context is the commandment to wear the *tzitzit,* the tassels we are to attach to the fringes of our garments.

In the first reference, the Hebrew verb is *latur* ("to scout"). The men are to scout the land and, ideally, to return with a report that would encourage the people to proceed with the conquest. At the conclusion of the reading, we are commanded to look at the *tzitzit* "and recall all the commandments of the Lord and observe them, so that you do not follow your heart and your eyes in your lustful urge." The Hebrew word for the verb "follow" is *taturu,* from the same root of *tur.*

So looking and seeing are important. And, somewhat sur-
prisingly, they are very complicated activities. The twelve spies
all "looked" at the same land, but they "saw" two very different
lands. Ten of them could only see the obstacles: the inhabitants
are powerful; the cities are fortified and large; the land is one
"that devours its settlers." Two of them saw a land that, with the
help of God, the Israelites could easily conquer (Num. 13:30–33).

How is it possible to "look" at the same data and "see" such
very different things? Easily. Because we see what we want to
see, what we are prepared to see, what we are educated to see.
Seeing is not purely objective. It is always influenced by our
inherent subjectivity, by what we bring to our seeing from ourselves. Thus Joshua and Caleb brought their faith in God's power
to their seeing of the land, whereas the ten others brought their
skepticism, their vulnerability, and their fears.

That's the purpose of the mitzvah of *tzitzit*. Precisely because
seeing is such a complicated affair, because we don't see what we
should see, or because we forget what we have seen, we must be
helped to see what our tradition would like us to see, and to
avoid seeing what we should not see. The expectation is that
when we see the *tzitzit*, we will not see in ways that we shouldn't
see. We will not follow the more "lustful urges of our eyes and
our hearts." Then, hopefully, we will remember "all the commandments of the Lord and observe them."

The *tzitzit*, then, are symbols. Their role is to point beyond
themselves. There are other such symbols in our tradition: the
rainbow after the flood, for example, or the various ritual foods
we consume at the Passover seder. In all of these instances, the
symbols convey, in a very concrete way, some deeper, much
more elusive truth. They are powerful educational tools.

Jewish faith, throughout the ages, was shaped by looking and
seeing. Jews did not reach an awareness of God through the use
of reason, medieval philosophers to the contrary notwithstand-
ing. Jews achieved that awareness by looking at nature and at

their distinctive history, and seeing both as transfigured by the presence of God. But like all seeing, this was a highly interpretive seeing, a seeing through a distinctive set of spectacles. That kind of seeing has to be trained, refined, and developed. The *tzitzit* are one of the strategies for achieving this kind of seeing.

The Holiness of
Yom HaAtzma'ut

THE MOST SIGNIFICANT ISSUE underlying our celebration of Yom HaZikaron (Israel Remembrance Day) and Yom HaAtzma'ut (Israel Independence Day) is the religious character of the days.

An informal survey of some Jewish calendars disclosed the following. A calendar distributed by a noted Israeli yeshivah notes simply that Wednesday, 5 Iyar, is Yom HaAtzma'ut. My Women's League for Conservative Judaism pocket calendar lists Tuesday, 4 Iyar, as Yom HaZikaron and Wednesday, 5 Iyar, as Yom HaAtzma'ut, and for the latter adds "Suggested Torah Reading Deuteronomy: 7:12–8:18" and "Suggested Haftarah: Isaiah 10:32–12:6." My synagogue calendar, which meticulously details all of the traditional liturgies and rituals for each day of the year, passes over both of these days in total silence.

The question is: Are we prepared to acknowledge that the creation of the State of Israel has a religious dimension—that it represents God's incursion into Jewish history and it therefore has to be celebrated in a distinctively religious, as opposed to a purely secular, manner? The range of practices described in my calendars reflects the various responses to that question within our community.

We know that from the beginning, Zionism was resisted by both our religious left and our religious right. Classical Reform objected because Zionism represented a reawakening of Jewish nationalism that the Reformers wanted to dampen. Ultra-Orthodoxy did so because Zionism was a secular movement that seemed to be forcing God's redemptive hand because the Messiah hadn't as yet arrived, and only the Messiah could bring an end to our exile. In our day, that resistance has been undoubtedly strengthened by the secular character of the State of Israel as we know it.

In time, the range of religious Jews who acknowledge the religious character of the event has broadened considerably. Reform in particular has done a complete turnabout and is now heavily invested in Israel, and much of Orthodoxy has recognized the miraculous—the term is only slightly hyperbolic—quality of the events our generation has been privileged to witness.

Yet questions persist. How should the birthday of the State of Israel be celebrated? For example, should we recite the Hallel psalms, as we do on other festivals? Should we recite them with a preliminary benediction that praises God for having commanded us to recite them on this day, as we do on other festivals?

Opinions differ. Some ignore the day, some recite Hallel with a benediction, some recite it without one. This last group points to the postbiblical nature of the event, claiming that God never explicitly commanded us to do anything in regard to this day. But they ignore the fact that God did not explicitly command us to recite Hallel on Chanukah, nor to light Chanukah candles, and yet all religious Jews do both with the appropriate benedictions because the Talmudic Rabbis accorded themselves the authority to read these events as God's work in history. Apparently our ancestors had this authority but, some believe, our own rabbinic leaders do not.

But the suggested Torah reading for Yom HaAtzma'ut would seem to offer us whatever mandate we need to establish its religious character. The centerpiece of that Torah reading tells us that "The Lord your God is bringing you into a good land, a land with streams and springs and fountains" (Deut. 8:7) and instructs us that we should "give thanks to the Lord your God for the good land which God has given you" (Deut. 8:10).

That we should praise God for our return to the land is also mandated in the suggested haftarah for the day. It is Isaiah's classical prophecy of redemption both national and universal: God will "hold up a signal to the nations and assemble the banished of Israel, and gather the dispersed of Judah from the four corners of the earth" (Isa. 11:12). And "the land shall be filled with devotion to the Lord as water covers the sea" (Isa. 11:9). On that day, we are to "praise the Lord, proclaim God's name. Make God's deeds known among the peoples; declare that God's name is exalted" (Isa. 12:4). What further mandate do we need?

This is the same haftarah we recite on the seventh day of Passover. The paradigms for our observance of Yom HaAtzma'ut, then, are Chanukah and Passover, our classic festivals of redemption. Yet the theological question remains: How do we know, beyond question, that God works in history? And when? We never know for sure. But that is precisely the test of faith that every religious person struggles with eternally. Religious Jews stake their lives on reading their personal and national experience through the spectacles of that faith. We believe that God does work in history, then and now.

That perspective seems to have had precious little impact in our day, both in Israel and in the United States as well. And it is fraught with tension and ambiguity because we also have to struggle with those moments when God's presence seems to be in eclipse. We must testify to that as well. Distinctive liturgies and rituals to celebrate the day have been slow to evolve, though the biblical readings are a notable beginning. But all of this takes time. It took centuries for our current celebrations of Chanukah and Passover to evolve.

In the meantime, our generation has witnessed momentous events, events that our ancestors for close to two millennia would have given anything to celebrate. We should grasp that opportunity.

Mundane Miracles

T HE STORY OF THE BIRTH of Samson is the haftarah for the Torah reading dealing with the institution of the *Nazir,* the ascetic who vows meticulously to abstain from wine, from contamination through contact with a corpse, and from cutting his hair.

The entire Samson story (Judg. 13–16) is rich in irony, not the least of which is that this man who was designated as a "*Nazarite* to God, from the womb to the day of his death," is ultimately destroyed by a woman's wiles. In fact, the entire narrative is structured around Samson's relationship with three women, the second of whom is explicitly identified as a whore. It is not surprising that the later tradition shows considerable discomfort with the institution of the *Nazir.* The Torah provides us with ample forbidden practices; we need not add to them.

However, this haftarah deals only with the story of Samson's birth. It has three dramatis personae: Samson's father, Manoach; his heretofore barren mother, who is unnamed; and an "angel of the Lord," who appears first to the woman and then to both parents to announce that this woman is to bear a child who will be a *Nazir* and who will be "the first to deliver Israel from the Philistines" (Judg. 13:5). Therefore the mother, too, must follow some of the laws of the *Nazir;* she must not drink wine or other intoxicants nor eat anything unclean.

Of the two parents, the unnamed mother is by far the more interesting. She is fully aware of the momentous nature of the experience. It is to her alone that the angel appears, twice; after the second time, she hastens to bring her husband to hear the message himself.

For his part, Manoach is totally out of touch with what is transpiring, for we are told that he is not aware that he is dealing with an angel. He is preoccupied with the mundane; he wants to play the gracious host and feed this man. He wants to know his name, so that he can honor him later "when your words come true" (Judg. 13:17). Only after the angel ascends in the flames of the sacrifice does Manoach appreciate what has happened, and he is consumed with dread: "We shall surely die, for we have seen a divine being" (Judg. 13:22). However, his wife, ever in touch with reality, reassures him. If God wanted to take our lives, why send us an angel, take our offering, and bring us this wonderful news?

Twice in this narrative we find the Hebrew root *pele*. When Manoach asks the angel for his name, the angel responds, "You must not ask for my name; it is *peli*," which JPS translates as "unknowable" (Judg. 13:18). A few verses later, Manoach and his wife offer a sacrifice, and as the flames leap up from the altar, we are told *"umafli la'asot."* JPS translates that as "a marvelous thing happened," and the angel ascended in the flames of the altar. For something or some event to be called *pele*, then, is to characterize it as beyond human understanding, wondrous, unknowable, even miraculous.

The phrase *umafli la'asot* was later detached from its original context and entered into the consciousness of the Jew through its use as the concluding phrase of a remarkable Talmudic benediction that we utter daily in the early morning liturgy. This short liturgical passage, commonly called the Asher Yatzar prayer, is also recited every time we perform our bodily functions. It praises God for having fashioned us with wisdom and creating us with many orifices and openings, so that should one be blocked when it is to be open, or opened when it is to be closed, "it would be impossible for us to survive and stand before You." Then we conclude, "Praised are you, Lord, who heals all flesh and acts wondrously [*umafli la'asot*]," the very phrase from our text.

Note the stunning association of these two words in our liturgy and their original use in the Samson story. In the story, they are used to describe nothing less than the angel's miraculous ascent in the flames of the sacrifice. In our liturgy, they are used to characterize the most mundane of our daily bodily functions.

Yet it is precisely that association that the tradition wants to highlight. The normal functioning of our body is as miraculous as the angel's ascent to heaven. We commonly ignore that association because we take our bodily functions for granted—until, of course, our bodies cease to function as we expect, and we are shocked into awareness of just how wondrously God has fashioned them.

Where do we find God? In the everyday, in the normal functioning of our bodies. Mistrust the Big Bang miracles. The world is filled with the presence of God, should we know where and how to look. Also, note the way in which our liturgy transforms a pithy biblical phrase in totally unanticipated ways in order to inform our religious sensibility. There is no richer source of Jewish theological inquiry than the liturgy.

Remembering to Remember

IN MY SIDDUR, after the concluding prayers of the daily Shacharit service—Aleinu, the psalm of the day, and the final Kaddish—I find a series of prayers and biblical passages called *Hosafot*, or "Additions."

The location of these passages, after the required service, seems to signify that their recitation is not strictly mandated but rather constitutes an extra measure of piety. My guess is that, typically, they are recited by those of us who do not have to dash off to work immediately following the service.

The first two of these are particularly interesting. The first is called the Six Remembrances, and the second is based on Maimonides' Thirteen Principles of Faith.

The Maimonides material concludes the introduction to his commentary on the tenth chapter of *Mishnah Sanhedrin,* called "Introduction to *Chelek*" because the Mishnah begins with the words "All Israel has a portion [*chelek*] in the age-to-come." The introduction as a whole deals with Maimonides' views on the doctrine of the age-to-come, and this list of thirteen principles constitutes the author's delineation of the minimal beliefs that all Jews must express if they are to merit eternal reward in the hereafter. A more familiar poetic version of these principles is the basis for the Yigdal hymn that we typically sing at the end of our Sabbath eve services.

Much of Maimonides' thinking was highly controversial, and this listing of principles of belief aroused particular debate. Thinkers objected to the very notion that Judaism insisted on such principles in the first place, to the number of principles Maimonides includes, to some specific principles, and to his formulation of the doctrines themselves.

In contrast, the Six Remembrances have no specific source. They are a pastiche of biblical verses, in five of which the Hebrew term *zachor*, "remember," appears, and in one its obverse, "Do not forget." What are we commanded to remember or not to forget? The Exodus from Egypt, the revelation at Sinai, Amalek, the episode of the Golden Calf, Miriam, the Sabbath?

One of these appears in Deuteronomy 24:8–9. This passage cautions us to follow the rulings of the priests in regard to skin afflictions, and then concludes: "Remember what the Lord your God did to Miriam on the journey, after you left Egypt." The association of Miriam, Moses' sister, with skin afflictions refers back to Miriam's punishment for having slandered her brother (Numbers 12). This episode is the basis for the ancient tradition that diseases of the skin are punishment for the sin of slander. This particular remembrance, then, is a warning against slandering our fellow humans.

Near the very end of the portion we are warned: "Remember what Amalek did to you on your journey after you left Egypt ... do not forget!" (Deut. 25:17–19). Amalek is Israel's archenemy, the prototype for Israel's persecutors throughout the generations. Amalek surprised us on the march after we left Egypt, when we were famished and weary, and cut down all our stragglers. Therefore we are to blot out the memory of Amalek from under heaven. As for the final admonition, "Do not forget!" (Deut: 25:19): We are commanded, then, to remember our persecutors, though how to reconcile remembering Amalek and blotting out its memory is another issue.

But the juxtaposition of Maimonides' thirteen principles and these six remembrances is fascinating, for they represent two different ways of establishing Jewish religious identity. Maimonides is the champion of the indispensability of authentic beliefs for Jewish authenticity. He begins his *Mishneh Torah*, the first comprehensive code of Jewish law that is designed to regulate Jewishly mandated behavior, with an entire book on what Jews are commanded to believe. For Maimonides, how is it even possible to behave as a Jew without the proper belief system in place? Hence his stipulation of basic principles of belief. That authentic beliefs are at the core of religious identity is the cornerstone of Christianity, with its tradition of dogmas and the locution of the credo ("I believe ...") at the heart of the traditional Christian mass.

But Judaism has always retained a healthy suspicion of theological abstractions. Abraham Joshua Heschel insists that ultimate religious convictions result not from conceptual thinking but from events, from moments of insight. Our faith is sustained by remembering those moments. Faith is not conceptual certainty but rather faithfulness to the moment of insight. That's why Heschel once said that he prefers the Six Remembrances over the Thirteen Principles.

If we need any convincing on the power of remembering, we should simply look about us at those of our beloved whose memory has vanished. Without memory, there is simply no identity. Our beings, our very existence, becomes fragmented. We literally no longer know who we are. If we want to know who we are as Jews, we must retain our collective Jewish memories.

Remember and Forget

WHY, IN THE DYNAMICS OF JEWISH MEMORY, is Egypt different than Amalek? Both of these peoples arouse painful
memories for us. Both oppressed our ancestors. Yet we are commanded to remember our redemption from Egypt but to blot out
the memory of Amalek.

The difference between these memories emerges in two
episodes in *Parashat Beshallach*. In the first, our ancestors have
crossed the sea in safety and, standing on dry land, they look
back and observe the pursuing Egyptian army drowning in the
sea. At this point, the midrash relates, the angels in heaven
sought to break forth in song, but God silenced them: "The work
of my hands are drowning in the sea and you want to sing
songs!"

To this day, at our Passover seder tables, we recall God's
mourning over the death of the Egyptians when we dip our fin-
gers in wine and shed a symbolic tear for each of the ten plagues
that God visited on them. And when we recite the Hallel psalms
in our synagogue during the last five days of the festival, we omit

two passages, again as a symbolic statement that our joy at our deliverance is muted because it was achieved through the death of many human beings, also God's creatures.

But the end of our Torah reading captures a very different tone. Here the enemy is Amalek. Here again, with God's intervention, the enemy is defeated in battle. This time, though, God's reaction is very different. God tells Moses, "Inscribe this in a document as a reminder, and read it aloud to Joshua: I will utterly blot out the memory of Amalek from under heaven" (Ex. 17:14). In Deuteronomy 25, we are commanded to remember what Amalek did to us on our journey after leaving Egypt and to "blot out the memory of Amalek from under heaven. Do not forget."

In a later biblical episode involving Amalek (I Sam. 15, the haftarah for the Sabbath prior to Purim, appropriately called Shabbat Zachor, the Sabbath of Remembering), King Saul has his kingship ripped from him precisely because he did not fulfill God's command to exterminate Amalek. Why the mourning over dead Egyptians and the fierce vengeance over Amalek?

Both Egypt and Amalek represent Israel's inveterate enemies. Yet nowhere in our classical literature is there the kind of venom directed against Egypt that we find directed against Amalek. We are intuitively much more comfortable with the "nice" God, the God who is filled with compassion and who mourns the death of even the Egyptian army. But it is worth remembering that the biblical image of God is not entirely "nice." The Bible often portrays God as capable of great rage and even what seems to us to be sheer cruelty, as, for example, in that disturbing first chapter of the book of Job.

But in the case of Amalek, one other factor seems to be operating. Look carefully at the context of the Amalek story in this portion, specifically at Exodus 17:1–7, the passage immediately prior to the Amalek story. This is the well-known narrative about the Israelites complaining about the lack of water. God commands Moses to take his staff and strike the rock, and the rock yields water. Whereupon we are told that the place where this occurred was named Massah and Meribah (literally "Trial and Quarrel") "because the Israelites quarreled and because they tried the Lord, saying, 'Is the Lord present among us or not?'" And then consider the verse immediately following: "Amalek came and fought with Israel at Rephidim."

The juxtaposition of such stories in the biblical narrative is never accidental. What it suggests here is that there is a deeper relationship between the two episodes. It would seem that God's anger here is appropriately directed not at Amalek but at Israel. This people has just been delivered from slavery. It has witnessed God's presence and power in Egypt and now, once again, at the sea. How is it even conceivable for them to ask "Is the Lord present among us or not?" God has every right to be angry at this point. Does God's presence have to be tested again and again?

God's anger, then, is at the fact of Israel's need to test God. God is not prepared to exterminate Israel, but God has to provide an eternal symbol of Israel's lack of faith. The symbol is Amalek. The story of our oppression at the hand of Egypt does not reflect our failures. Amalek does. This is why we are commanded to remember Amalek forever. That Amalek is a symbol is borne out by the fact that though we are commanded to exterminate the memory of Amalek, in truth Amalek remains very much alive in our memories to this day. First, we read the story of Amalek twice in each year's Torah cycle, and we recall it again in the haftarah before Purim. More interesting, the name of Amalek has been used to refer to Israel's enemies, generation after generation.

Finally, and even more significantly, the Deuteronomy passage that commands us to blot out the memory of Amalek also tells us to remember what Amalek did to us on our journey out of Egypt. What is it then? Are we to remember? Or are we to blot out the memory? How can we do both?

We can do both if we recall that Amalek is a symbol of our inherent lack of faith in God. We are commanded both to remember and to blot out the reason why we are commanded to remember. Paradoxically, if we don't remember that reason, we are condemned never to succeed in blotting out the memory of Amalek.

PART II

Images of God

The Divine Wrath

A BIBLICAL PASSAGE FOUND IN NUMBERS 31 has haunted the sensibility of thinking and feeling Jews for centuries. In this chapter, God commands Moses to wreak vengeance upon the Midianites for having incited their women to seduce the Israelites into the pagan worship of Baal Peor (as described earlier in Numbers 25). An army is dispatched and wins a glorious victory; the Midianite males and their kings are all killed, and the women, children, herds, and spoils are brought back to Moses.

But Moses is enraged. "You have spared every female! Yet they are the very ones who ... induced the Israelites to trespass against the Lord.... Now therefore slay every male among the children, and slay also every woman who has known a man carnally" (Num. 31:14–17). Presumably the command is carried out, and the rest of the chapter deals with the ritual purification of the soldiers (because of their contact with death) and the division of the booty.

We cannot read this chapter without recalling a similar incident recorded in I Samuel 15. Here the prophet Samuel commands

King Saul to exact vengeance against the Amalekites for having attacked Israel on its way out of Egypt (Ex. 17:8–15), in fulfillment of God's command (in Deut. 25:17–19) to "blot out the memory of Amalek." This time, in contrast to the story of the Midianites, the charge is specific: "Spare no one, but kill alike men and women, infants and sucklings, oxen and sheep, camels and asses!" (I Sam. 15:3).

Saul and the Israelite army emerge triumphant but choose to spare King Agag of Amalek, the best of the animals, and all else that is of value. Samuel is enraged that God's charge was flouted. Because of this disobedience, Saul's kingship is taken from him and his family, eventually to be passed on to David.

What are we to make of these stories? A piece of us is clearly disturbed by this image of a God who demands such total and bloody vengeance, who insists that even women and animals must be extirpated.

In the case of the Midianites, the Bible goes out of its way to anticipate our discomfort and to try to justify the decree. It was precisely the women who were the cause of Israel's descent into pagan worship; that's why they specifically must be killed. But is this sufficient cause? And what about the Amalekite animals? And how do we square this image with that touching concluding verse of the book of Jonah, where God emerges as profoundly sensitive to the fate of the inhabitants and animals of Nineveh?

The case of Amalek seems to have a character of its own. Amalek symbolizes absolute evil. They attacked the Israelites when they were most vulnerable, when they were "famished and weary" (Deut. 25:18). Absolute evil is to be absolutely destroyed. Not even the animals, not even the spoils are to remain. Vengeance must be complete. Our generation is painfully familiar with this feeling.

In the case of the Midianites, the midrash seems to have felt a similar discomfort, specifically in regard to Moses' anger. The Rabbis note that it was Elazar, the High Priest, who communicated the laws of purification to the soldiers returning from the war. Why Elazar and not Moses? Because Moses' rage led him to forget about the laws of purification, and Elazar made up for Moses' forgetfulness. But what about God's anger?

The emotion of anger is always disturbing. There is an anarchic quality to anger; we feel it as a loss of control and we tend to want to rein it in. That leads us to feel a similar disquiet about God's anger. Shouldn't God be above anger? Above vengeance? It is precisely this image of God that has led Christians throughout the centuries to contrast the angry God of the Hebrew scriptures with the loving God of Christianity.

This is clearly an oversimplification. The God of the Hebrew scriptures knows and feels compassion and love—for the widow, the orphan, the oppressed, the slave, for Israel even when it has sinned, and, as Jonah reminds us, for Nineveh, "that great city in which there are more than 120,000 persons who do not yet know their right hand from their left, and many beasts as well" (Jonah 4:11).

Yet this same God is capable of great anger, and, as the late Rabbi Abraham Heschel perceives (in a central chapter of his book *The Prophets*), we tend to be embarrassed by that image. But, Heschel reminds us, divine anger is never unpredictable, irrational, or reckless. It is always voluntary, purposeful, motivated by a clear moral sense, an expression of God's concern for humanity, more a matter of righteous indignation.

A God who is incapable of being angry, then, is an indifferent God, and to Heschel, both in his theology and in his own social and political activity, indifference is the ultimate sin. "Is it more compatible with our conception of the grandeur of God," Heschel asks, "to claim that God is emotionally blind to the misery of man rather than profoundly moved?"

We return to these biblical passages, then, with a sharper awareness of their ambiguities. We must remember that all of our images of God represent partial projections of our own human sensibilities. Our ancestors did that, and we continue the process today, sometimes with discordant results. That's why certain biblical texts create tension within us. We are clearly much more comfortable with an image of God as totally loving and forgiving, because we feel that we should be that way, too.

But is not righteous indignation in the face of outrageous behavior a totally legitimate reaction, for us and for God? And just as we are aware of the difference between feeling anger and acting on it, so is God. Sometimes, as with Nineveh, God conquers the anger; sometimes, as with Amalek and Midian, God doesn't. That is a complex and difficult decision, for us and for God, and we may not always agree.

Testing God

THAT THE STORY OF THE *AKEDAH*, the binding of Isaac, represents an awesome test of Abraham's faith is clear. Implicit in
the narrative, however, is that not only is Abraham being tested,
but God is being tested as well. That is the only way we can make
sense of one of the many mysteries that abound in this stunning
narrative: Abraham's silence in the face of God's command.

We in the Western tradition have been trained to think of
God as ultimate perfection. This "God of the philosophers" has
it all together; God is all-powerful and all-knowing, the actualization of all potentialities. God has no failings, no lacks, no
needs. This philosophical image of God is far removed from that
of the biblical God. There, the image is of God's persistent
frustration and failure. De jure, God may be the absolute sovereign of all of creation whose will is ultimate. But de facto, from
the early Genesis stories through the Israelite rebellions in the
desert to the end of prophetic literature, God's will and hopes for
civilization are constantly flouted. This sovereign is singularly

incapable of realizing almost any of the expectations God has for creation.

This limitation in the biblical God is not one of essence. The biblical God is not intrinsically limited. Rather, it is the result of God's will, of commitments God has freely entered into.

First, God created human beings to be free, and the actualization of human freedom becomes the greatest challenge to God's power. Second, we are told in God's momentous debate with Abraham over the fate of Sodom and Gomorrah, of God's commitment to a specific "way of the Lord" that involves doing "what is just and right" (Gen. 18:19). Yet it is precisely this mutual commitment to doing "what is just and right" that gives Abraham the right to challenge God's decision to obliterate the two cities.

Look at Moses' intercession with God after the incident of the Golden Calf: God is prepared to destroy the Israelites as punishment for their sin. But Moses counters with two claims: First, what will the Egyptians say if you destroy this people? Second, remember your promise to the patriarchs that you would make this people as numerous as the stars in the heavens.

Astonishingly, God renounces the punishment. This is hardly the behavior of a sovereign God! Where is God's omnipotence? But the pattern remains the same throughout the biblical narrative. God's expectations are clear, but they are constantly frustrated. Frustration leads to anger, then to regret, then to infinite yearning, and ultimately to renewal. And then the pattern begins again.

Twenty generations separate Adam from Abraham. Only once throughout these generations does the Bible choose to designate a human being a *tzaddik,* a righteous man. It soon becomes clear, however, that this *tzaddik,* Noah, hardly represents an enduring paradigm of righteousness. What does this record tell us about God's ability to inspire righteousness or genuine devotion?

Then along comes Abraham, who has been called faithful. As Abraham's career is about to end, God feels the need to put this devotion to the ultimate test. Sure, the test will determine the strength of Abraham's loyalty, but in the process, it will also test God's ability to inspire the kind of loyalty that will stand as a paradigm for the generations. From here on, God will be able to point to Abraham as the model of what God can expect of a human being and of what a human being can achieve.

On some level of awareness, Abraham understands what is at stake here. That's why he utters not a word of challenge. Abraham knows full well that he has the grounds for such a challenge. He, too, as Moses would later do, could invoke God's promises for his posterity. He could also remind God of their mutual commitment to doing what is "just and right," for it was clear both to God and to Abraham that this command was hardly "just and right."

But Abraham does neither, for to do so might compromise the starkness of the trial. How would God respond to such a challenge? Negotiate, as in the case of the evil cities? Withdraw, as God would do after the Golden Calf? But how would either of these scenarios serve as the climactic moment in Abraham's career?

So Abraham utters not a word of protest. What was in Abraham's mind during that fateful three-day journey? First, that there was no question but that he would pass this test as he had passed other tests. Second, that in so doing, he would vindicate God's choosing him as the exemplar of human faithfulness. Third, he hoped, that once vindicated, God too would, freely and without negotiation, do "what is just and right" and spare his son. For indeed there was another dimension to this testing of God. If God was to be reassured about what kind of man Abraham was, Abraham also needed to reassure himself as to what kind of god this God was. Was this a God who kept promises?

Was this God truly committed to doing "what is just and right"?
Was this God truly unique among the gods?

To Abraham, if this was a God who would expect a father to
sacrifice his son, then what was the point of his entire career of
loyalty? Indeed, what was the point of sparing his son? Much
was at stake in this encounter, then, and, to the greater glory of
Abraham and God, much was resolved.

The Rebuke

T WO EXAMPLES OF *TOCHECHAH*, literally "rebuke," are found in the Torah. The first is found in Leviticus 26:14–45 and is an extended and very graphic description of the punishments God will visit upon the Israelites should they choose not to obey God and God's commandments. The second, and even longer *tochechah*, is found in Deuteronomy 28.

In the liturgical reading of the Torah, both of these passages are commonly read quickly and in an undertone. No one wants to dwell on these prophecies, most of which, incidentally, have proven in the course of our history to be painfully accurate. There is, however, one major difference between the two passages. In Deuteronomy, the message is unrelieved doom and disaster. In Leviticus, however, a glimmer of potential consolation is allowed to emerge. God promises that in the midst of Israel's sufferings, God will remember the covenant with Abraham, Isaac, and Jacob; the covenant with the community of the Exodus; and the land. However harsh the punishment, God will not utterly destroy the Israelites and annul God's covenant with them.

Our consolation, then, lies in the *brit,* in the covenant. Theologically, this is an extraordinarily powerful claim. It is the covenant that, so to speak, binds God's hands. This omnipotent God, whose power is unquestioned, freely chooses not to exercise that power. God's own promises simply preclude that outcome. It is that irreversible covenant that gives us the right to make demands and to entertain expectations from, and even to challenge, God. It is precisely the covenant that assures us of God's eternal concern for us. That is why two of these verses (Lev. 26:42 and 45) are quoted in our Rosh HaShanah Musaf liturgy as part of the Zichronot, or "Remembering," passages. At the time of year when we turn to God for forgiveness, we remind God of the covenant that guarantees that our prayers will be answered.

Note also that God's limited power is not God's essence, but God's choice. This is not a precursor of some current notions of a God whose limited power is a matter of God's very nature. God's nature, here, remains all-powerful, except when God chooses not to be. It is as if the greatest manifestation of God's power lies precisely in the ability to curb that power.

What is most interesting about this passage, however, is not what it says about our sources of consolation, but rather what it does not say. In the perspective of Judaism's later development, this notion of God's grace flowing to us because of the covenant is expanded to include the power of *teshuvah,* or repentance, specifically preemptive repentance, the kind of repentance that will lead God to forget about imposing any punishment at all. True, Leviticus 26:41 alludes to the fact that in the midst of its misery, Israel will atone for its iniquity, and then God will remember the covenant—after the punishment has been meted out. In contrast, the kind of repentance advocated throughout prophetic literature cancels out beforehand any punishment that is to come as a result of our sins.

Jeremiah 18 is a striking illustration of this notion of preemptive repentance. The prophet is commanded to go visit a potter and observe how the potter can decide that if the pot he is in the process of making is spoiled, he can simply discard it and make a new one. Such is the fate of Israel in the hands of God. "Just like clay in the hands of the potter, so are you in My hands, O house of Israel" is a theme echoed in one touching *piyut* in the Yom Kippur evening service. Like the potter, God too can decree that a nation is to be destroyed. But should that nation turn back from its wickedness, God can change its curse to a blessing, and vice versa.

The image, then, is of an all-powerful God whose plans for a people are shaped by the behavior of that people. God's decision depends on our own. We have the power to determine our fate. That gift is part of God's grace to us. To concretize that message, the book of Jonah, which we read on Yom Kippur, teaches us of the preemptive power of repentance. Jonah himself did not understand the full power of his own prophecy, but God was willing to change Nineveh's fate from disaster to blessing simply because of the people's genuine repentance.

It is interesting to speculate how and why this theme of the preemptive power of repentance made its way into prophetic literature. A clue is supplied by Psalm 103, verses 7–13, which describe how totally and utterly compassionate God is in the face of our sins, how God has the power to remove our sins "as east is far from west." Why? Verse 14 provides the answer: Because God knows how we are formed; God is mindful that we are dust. Why, then, is God so ready to forgive us, even before God punishes? Simply because God is responsible for the way we are. Why, then, should our repentance not be acceptable?

This first example from Leviticus of *tochechah* is an extraordinary example of Jewish theology in the process of development, from an image of God as open to repentance after punishment, to one of God eager to accept our repentance even before punishment.

Now, God waits for us.

Unshakable Covenant

THE FIRST TEN VERSES from Isaiah 54 encompass a network of themes that are absolutely indispensable for our self-understanding as Jews. Recall that these verses are part of one of the seven *haftarot* of consolation that lead us from the mourning of Tisha B'Av to the solemnity of Rosh HaShanah. The theme of consolation is indeed central throughout. The barren one, Zion, is no longer childless; she must shout in exultation, for she will become exceedingly fruitful, and her children will populate the towns that are now desolate. The days of shame are behind her, for God, the Lord of Hosts, will redeem her as the wife of God's youth.

True, for a brief moment, God's face has been hidden in anger, but that was just momentary. For as God once vowed that the waters of the flood will never again consume the land, so God promises that never again will God rebuke Zion. Finally, the powerful peroration: "For the mountains may move, and the hills be shaken, but My loyalty shall never move from you, nor My covenant of friendship be shaken, said the Lord, who takes you back in love."

There is much here to ponder. First, the notion of God's "hiding of the face" as a metaphor for Israel's sense of abandonment by God is central to biblical theology. Frequently, God's abandonment of Israel is punishment for Israel's having abandoned God; sometimes (as in another miniature biblical gem, Psalm 13) it is simply inexplicable, one phase of the dynamic of God's interpersonal relationship with human beings.

In modern Jewish thought, this theme is taken up by Martin Buber, who uses the term "eclipse of God" to deal with the theological implications of the Holocaust. The hiding of God's face in anger is the obverse of the turning of God's countenance toward us (as in the blessing of the *kohanim* in Num. 6:25–26) in favor and blessing. We turn toward those we love as a sign of favor; we turn away from them in anger and frustration. Everyone has felt similar moments in our relationships with those we love. We have also felt moments of God's absence, as we have felt God's palpable presence at other times in our lives. In Buber's terminology, it is the "I-It" phase of our relationship with God, the obverse of the "I-Thou" experience, when God is immediately present to us.

The implication of that dynamic dimension to our relationship with God is that no human being can ever rest comfortably with the sense that his or her faith in God is secure and permanent. But the prophet assures us that so is God's eclipse. "For a little while," God forsook us: "In slight anger, for a moment, I hid My face from you." In contrast, "with kindness everlasting I will take you back in love."

What is permanent is God's covenant: with nature and the world, after the flood; and with Israel, beginning with Abraham and confirmed again at Sinai. Both covenants bind God. They are even more permanent and stable than the seemingly unshakable mountains. The mountains may be dislodged, but God's promise to Israel will never be shaken. In brief moments it may appear to be forgotten, but in reality it is as firm, steadfast, and permanent as possible.

The covenant is the linchpin of our relationship with God, the core of our self-awareness as Jews. It gives us the framework through which we can challenge God in regard to God's own commitments to us. Without the covenant, as Elie Wiesel reminds us, we have no grounds for our challenge to God. With it, we have a claim. There is no need to underline the centrality of this theme as we struggle to understand our generation's life experience as Jews.

More important, the covenant, a legalistic or jurisprudential metaphor, is itself an expression of a far more profound theme—God's everlasting affection for Israel. The prophet portrays God as Israel's youthful suitor and Israel as the bride of God's youth. God's covenant with Israel will never be shaken because God loves Israel; we will always be taken back "in love."

It is this passage's theme of God's affection-laden commitments to us that properly links Tisha B'Av with Rosh HaShanah. As a testament of consolation, the passage reminds us that our national disasters should never be understood as a radical break in God's relationship with Israel. As an anticipation of the solemnity of the *Yamim Nora'im*, it reminds us that we can always turn back to God in repentance and be confident of God's eternal promises of renewal and redemption.

During this time period, every weekday morning we hear the sound of the shofar, and twice daily we recite Psalm 27. The panic we feel when we experience the hiding of God's face is on our lips. "Do not hide Your face from me ... You have ever been my help. Do not forsake me, do not abandon me ..." (Ps. 27:9). Rather, "Show me Your way ... and lead me on a level path" (Ps. 27:11). But if God is to turn toward us in blessing, then we too must turn back to God. Therefore, "Look to the Lord; be strong and of good courage! O look to the Lord" (Ps. 27:14).

Symbol or Idol

O F THE MANY STRANGE TALES that are found throughout the book of Numbers, few are stranger than the story of the copper serpent (Num. 21:5–9). Again, we are told, the Israelites murmur against Moses and God, and again, God punishes, this time by sending a plague of *seraph* (burning or poisonous) serpents. Many of the people die from their bite. Again the people repent and ask Moses to intercede on their behalf. God then instructs Moses to make a *"seraph* figure" and mount it on a standard. Moses builds a copper serpent and mounts it on a standard, and whoever looks at the figure is cured.

What are we to make of this strange story? On the face of it, this is an example of homeopathic magic, where the image of an object is used to manipulate the object itself. In an excursus on this story in Rabbi Jacob Milgrom's Jewish Publication Society commentary to Numbers, we are given numerous examples of pictures of copper serpents from antiquity. These pictures served as amulets that were used to cure snakebites. We also know that to this day, the serpent is the symbol for healing.

The later fate of Moses' copper serpent is equally fascinating. It apparently remained within the Israelite community and was probably erected in the court of the Temple, where it could be worshipped as a source of healing. That's why in II Kings 18:4, we are told that it was destroyed by King Hezekiah (one of the rare "good" kings in Israel's later history) as part of his religious reform, "for until that time the Israelites had been offering sacrifices to it; it was called *Nehushtan*" (a play on the Hebrew word *nehoshet*, "copper"). Milgrom notes that in Canaanite religion, the snake was regarded as a symbol of life and fertility. It was thus familiar to the Israelites and could easily become used for pagan worship. In other words, what began as a symbol of God's charitable concern for Israel eventually became an idol replacing God, and thus it had to be destroyed.

That is undoubtedly why the rabbinic traditions of this story spiritualize the entire episode. According to the Rabbis, the point of the story was not that the Israelites should look at the copper serpent itself, but rather that they should direct their gaze on high, to God, who alone has the power to heal, "for can a serpent kill or can a serpent heal?" (*Mishnah Rosh HaShanah* 3:8). The copper serpent was thus a means and not an end, a symbol for God and not the reality itself. Quite properly, then, when a symbol replaces or overshadows the reality it is designed to stand for, it becomes an idol and must be destroyed.

Why, then, did God not simply heal the bitten Israelites without the copper serpent? Why use this device? Why create a symbol that always runs the risk of becoming idolized in the first place? The obvious answer is that symbols for God are simply indispensable. That is inherent in the very nature of the biblical God who totally transcends the familiar natural order, who cannot be seen, touched, or manipulated by people. If God is to enter into our communal religious life, we simply must create appropriate symbols for God's presence, and then we inevitably run the risk that these symbols will cease to function as symbols and replace that which they were created to point to. They have then subverted their original purpose and must be destroyed.

What is fascinating about Judaism, especially in light of the later interpretation of this story, is that we are forbidden to create visual symbols for God. We do, however, use countless conceptual symbols for God. God is our Shepherd, we say, our King, Parent, Judge, Healer. None of these has inherent sanctity. God is not "really"—that is, objectively or literally—any of these. Rather, these terms serve as concrete representations designed to reveal God's reality, which infinitely eludes all concretizations. Without them, we would bereft of ways to speak, think, or even begin to understand God.

But every symbol exists in a state of tension. It is indispensable but it inevitably runs the risk of losing its status as a symbol and becoming itself the Ultimate. At that point, it becomes an idol. The proper definition of idolatry is the act of elevating to ultimacy that which is itself less than ultimate. It is the cardinal sin.

We cannot read the story of the copper serpent without associating it with another serpent, the one in the Genesis story of Adam and Eve. That serpent is radically different from this one. Here, the serpent is a source of healing. The Genesis serpent is the source of evil and rebellion against God.

There is no clearer evidence of the symbolic character of these serpents than the fact that they can serve two such radically different purposes. The serpent itself is a source of neither healing nor evil. It acquires its symbolic character by its context, by the way it is used in a community's liturgical life. The message of this story is that we must create religious symbols and we must also mistrust them.

Face to Face with God

S O GOD HAS A FACE! That seems to be the implication of the latter two blessings of the *kohanim* that we find in Numbers 6:22–27, part of *Parashat Naso,* which together with the Shema and the Decalogue are arguably the most often quoted passages in the Torah. These two blessings read, "May God's face shine on you and be gracious to you" and "May God lift God's countenance on you and grant you peace." In both cases, the Hebrew reads *panav,* literally God's "face."

Of course, God does not really have a face because God is not embodied. When applied to God, the notion of God's face has to be understood as metaphorical, as are the other references to God's facial features implied in the notion that God "sees," "hears," "speaks," and even, in the Noah story, "smells" (Gen. 8:21). None of these should be understood as implying that God literally has eyes, ears, a mouth, or a nose. They are all metaphors, or anthropomorphisms, literally, the attribution of human forms to God.

But the more expansive notion that God has a face suggests a different set of associations. Think of what we experience when we see another person's face. First, the face confers identity. When we see a person's face, we recognize who that person is, what makes that person different from other people. To look a person in the face is also to enter into a relationship with that person. In contrast, we are frequently aware of people who avoid looking at us in the face, who look "through" us, who clearly don't wish to relate to us.

Second, and even more important, the face reflects feelings. The face carries the smile or the frown, which betrays whether that person is pleased or angry, or more generally, concerned for us. The range of human emotions is conveyed by the look on the face.

Apart from the reference in Numbers, there are other biblical texts that refer to God's face. For example, there are the various references to God's relationship to Moses. In Exodus 33:17–23, Moses asks to behold God's "Presence." But God responds that Moses may see God's "back"—of course, also a metaphor—but not God's "face," for "man may not see Me and live." Note here that seeing God's "face" is the same as seeing "Me." The face is the person. But after Moses' death, the Torah tells us that Moses was distinctive among the prophets because, in contrast to the other prophets, "The Lord singled him out, face to face" (Deut. 34:10).

The tension between these two texts reflects the ambiguity of any human being's relationship to God. In the first of these passages, Moses wants to be reassured of God's continuing concern for Israel; the context of the passage is the Golden Calf episode. Here God's response is decidedly ambiguous.

However, the second passage reflects the unique kind of intimacy that characterized God's relation to Moses himself. To be "face to face" with another person is to have that kind of intense interpersonal relation that Martin Buber was later to call an "I-Thou" relationship. That is the kind of relationship Moses clearly enjoyed.

Another reference is to a phrase that appears many times in the Torah and in prophetic texts, the claim that God "will hide God's face" either from Israel or from an individual. God's hiding of the face frequently is an expression of God's anger at Israel's sinfulness, as in Deuteronomy 31:17. At other times, however, as in Psalm 13:2, it indicates God's mysterious, inexplicable absence, the psalmist's sense of being abandoned by God, apparently without cause, leaving the author lonely, vulnerable, and terrified. The hiding of God's face indicates God's absence, the void left by a dramatic break in the relationship with God. That sense of God's sudden, inexplicable absence from our lives is also familiar to every believer.

Finally, the two references to God's face in the blessings of the *kohanim* should be understood as the very obverse of God's hidden face. In Psalm 13, the psalmist, painfully experiencing God's absence, pleads: "Look at me! Answer me!" Now we are promised first that God will look at us, will see us, will relate to us, and deal favorably with us; and in the last blessing, we are assured that God will grant us *shalom,* which means "peace" and much more—harmony, contentment, wholeness. To see God's face is to be aware of God's concern, or even more, of God's love. It is then easy to understand why we recite this passage as frequently as we do. It expresses God's ultimate blessing.

The God of Jonah

I NVARIABLY, YEAR AFTER YEAR, the Selichot service we recite the Saturday prior to Rosh HaShanah plunges me into the High Holy Days mood. Of course, I know what the calendar is telling me; and of course, I have heard the shofar again. But Selichot is very special. Part of the story is the glorious music, the distinctive High Holy Days melodies that we will hear for the first time this year when the cantor chants the opening Half Kaddish. Equally important are the words of the liturgy that convey the season's distinctive theological message: Our God is a forgiving God.

That image of God is in stark contrast to the image of God that we encounter in the closing chapters of Deuteronomy. This is a God who threatens to punish God's people should they worship other gods. That punishment is portrayed in vivid terms: plagues, diseases, sulfur, and salt—just like God's punishment of Sodom and Gomorrah, we are told. God's chosen people will be treated like the Bible's two paradigmatic evil cities. That is quite a statement.

There is but one reference in this Torah text to a softer image of God, a God who is prepared to accept the people's repentance and welcome them back with love. But this reference (Deut. 30:1–5) makes clear that God's readiness to forgive can take place only after the punishment has been meted out. Then, if we return to God and heed God's command, God will welcome us back. Here, repentance can only follow punishment. The possibility that repentance might preempt God's punishment is unknown here.

Yet preemptive repentance is everywhere in prophetic theology, and it is this prophetic God image that pervades the Selichot liturgy. The contrast is particularly striking because, paradoxically, the Selichot service is centered around a Torah text from Exodus that we recite again and again, throughout the Selichot service and again on Yom Kippur. But the version of this text that we recite on these occasions has already been subjected to an intrabiblical, prophetic midrash that effectively turns its original meaning on its head. In the process, the punitive God of our Torah reading becomes the all-compassionate God of the prophets.

The Torah text is Exodus 34:6–7. It has come to be known as the Thirteen Attributes because it lists thirteen distinctive attributes, or characteristics, of God. I have referred frequently to this text's cumulative portrait of God as a mixed bag because it begins with a description of God as compassionate, gracious, slow to anger, and filled with loving-kindness; but as the passage continues, the image turns darker. This God "does not remit all punishment." In fact, this God "visits the iniquity of fathers upon children and children's children, upon the third and fourth generation."

At Selichot, however, we do not recite this entire passage. Instead, we recite an amended version that omits the concluding, darker side of the God image, retaining only the opening, brighter side. We recite this version as opposed to the original because the High Holy Days prophetic book par excellence, the book of Jonah, the haftarah for the Yom Kippur Minchah service, has already amended the text.

Jonah is our only successful prophet. He prophecies, Nineveh repents, and punishment is averted. But Jonah is furious at God for having spared the city, and he rages that this is precisely why he first tried to evade God's mission. He knew that Nineveh would repent, the city would be spared, and he would be thought a false prophet.

How did Jonah know that the city would be spared? Because he knew the description of God in Exodus and, in addressing God (Jonah 4:2), he uses those very words, but only the opening ones: "I know," Jonah said, "that You are a compassionate and gracious God, slow to anger, abounding in kindness," a blatant quotation from Exodus 34. Then, in place of the darker, concluding words of that Exodus passage, Jonah's own concluding words are "renouncing punishment," the very opposite of the Exodus warning, "Yet He does not remit all punishment."

On Selichot, and throughout the High Holy Days period, it is the Jonah version of the passage that we recite, not the Exodus version. We pray to Jonah's forgiving God, a God who welcomes the repentance that comes before punishment and successfully defers God's rage. As Nineveh was spared, so will we be spared. And we assume that every Jew who enters the Selichot service and the High Holy Days season has already done the work of repentance.

Arguing with God

ON THREE OCCASIONS IN MOSES' final address to Israel, prior to his death and Israel's entering the Promised Land, Moses mentions that he prayed to God on Israel's behalf for forty days and forty nights.

The broader context is a review of the Golden Calf episode. Moses acts as an intercessor on behalf of Israel, trying to persuade God to refrain from punishing the people. The tone is set when God, observing the Israelites worshiping the Calf, cries out: "Let Me alone and I will destroy them and blot out their name from under heaven" (Deut. 9:14).

"Let Me alone!" Or, more colloquially, "Let Me at them!" God needs Moses' permission to punish Israel? It is just as in Genesis 18, when God shares with Abraham the divine plan to destroy Sodom and Gomorrah. In both instances, we are given a peek into God's private deliberations. In both cases, humans are informed of God's impulse to punish. But then, why ask for permission? This all-powerful God needs human consent before acting?

But of course, God does need human consent; the biblical God's power is tied up in constraints of God's own making. God knows that Israel merits punishment, and God has the power to punish. But at the same time God hopes, and is even eager, that Moses and Abraham will intercede. Moses must have picked up this nuance because he then formulates three arguments (Deut. 9:26–29) to persuade God not to act punitively.

The first appeals to God's longstanding relationship with Israel: "Do not annihilate Your very own people, whom You redeemed in Your majesty." The phrase "Your very own people" is a direct challenge to God's earlier reference to Israel as "the people whom you [i.e., Moses] brought out of Egypt" (Deut. 9:12). Moses reminds God that Israel is even more God's people than his. This intimacy can tolerate infractions of the relationship.

The second appeals to God's relationship with the patri-archs, specifically the divine promise made to Abraham, Isaac, and Jacob that their posterity would be beyond number and would inherit the land. In other words, God's hands are tied by promises God has made in earlier times. So much for God's vaunted power and freedom! Sure, God is free and powerful, except when God has forsworn both freedom and unlimited power, as is the case here.

The third argument is the most daring. Here, Moses appeals to God's concern for God's public image: "Else the country from which You freed us (note "us," not "them") will say, 'It was because the Lord was powerless to bring them into the Land that He had promised them, and because He rejected them that He brought them out to have them die in the wilderness.'" This last argument is nothing short of blackmail. It recalls the admoni-tion that some of us used to hear in our childhood to the effect that Jews have to act in a more elevated, moral way—otherwise, "What will the Christians think?" But should God be concerned with God's image in the world?

Moses' appeal is scandalous but also brilliant, for, after all, one of God's motives for redeeming Israel in the first place is precisely so the nations of the world will acknowledge God's power and majesty. The appeal, then, is to God's own, oft-stated concerns and hopes. If God really cares about God's public image, then God has to preserve Israel. Moses' brief on behalf of Israel ends on the note of intimacy: "Yet they are Your very own [not only "my"] people." A few verses later, Moses quotes God's reaction (Deut. 10:10–11): God "heeded me once again; the Lord agreed not to destroy you. And the Lord said to me, 'Up, resume the march at the head of the people, that they may go in and possess the land that I swore to their fathers to give them.'"

God wants to be dissuaded from punishing. That's why God asks Moses to "let Me at them!"—and the prophet's honorable task is precisely to intercede, as Abraham interceded on behalf of the righteous in Sodom and Gomorrah, and as Samuel and the other prophets did in their own day. Psalm 106:23 captures the thrust of the prophetic role: God would have destroyed Israel, "had not Moses, God's chosen one, confronted God in the breach to avert God's destructive wrath."

The image of God in this text is far from the conventional one. God deliberates what to do. God is ambivalent, torn between conflicting impulses; God wants to be persuaded to constrain God's own claim that sin must be punished. God's mind is open to change.

We, too, come before God with our prayers for health and blessing. But in pleading before God, we know that God is singularly vulnerable to our prayers because of God's longstanding intimacy with Israel, because of God's own promises to our ancestors, and even because this omnipotent God still worries about public opinion. Moses has given us a singularly powerful and effective brief with which we, too, can confront God.

Schoenberg's Midrash
on the Golden Calf

Recall that Moses and Aaron were brothers; that Aaron was appointed to be Moses' mouthpiece, putting God's teaching into words that human beings could grasp; and that it was Aaron who built the Golden Calf while Moses was up on the mountain, receiving the Torah and the twin tablets.

The tension between the brothers surfaces in the narrative of the Golden Calf episode, but it was inherent in their relationship from the start. Moses was the prophet, thoroughly and exclusively committed to God, to a transcendent, demanding, and incomprehensible Reality. Aaron was the mediator. His function was to bring this distant God into the daily life experience of the human community. But how is it even possible to give a human face to this God without betraying God?

Aaron was also the first High Priest, the officiant at the sacrificial rituals in the desert sanctuary. The very presence of a sanctuary, or later of the Temple, with its attendant rituals, was very much a physical, visual symbol of God's presence within the community. In the later tradition, Aaron was known as one who sought harmony, pursued it, and attracted people to Torah. In all of these roles, Aaron was God's supreme mediator.

These thoughts were occasioned by my attendance at a performance of the Metropolitan Opera's production of Arnold Schoenberg's *Moses und Aaron*. It was an extraordinary experience that has transformed my understanding of the Golden Calf story and the tension between the brothers.

Those familiar with the opera, ignore for now the composer's use of a twelve-tone scale; the music sounded strange to my layman's ears. But the core of the opera is Schoenberg's libretto, an elaborate midrash on the biblical story. And at the heart of the midrash is a series of tension-filled dialogues between the two brothers on how to relate to God.

The first words of the opera define Moses' position: "Only One, infinite, thou omnipresent One, unperceived and inconceivable God!" Aaron's response some moments later is, "Can you love what you dare not even conceive?"

There it is, that unavoidable tension in all human attempts to relate to God. The problem is, both are right. Moses is right because it is of the very essence of the monotheistic God to be totally beyond human comprehension; that's what makes the Lord God and not a big human being. To believe that God can be adapted to the human mind and human language is to commit the sin of idolatry. It is effectively a betrayal of God.

But Aaron is also right because how can this absolute, transcendent God touch and transform human lives, intervene in history, care about orphans and widows, and be worshiped? How can this God be loved by human beings? In the third act of the opera (which Schoenberg never set to music), Aaron comments on the brothers' dispute: "I was to speak in images while you spoke in ideas; I was to speak to the heart, you to the mind." Both are indispensable.

But Schoenberg's most stunning midrashic twist on the biblical narrative occurs when Moses comes down from the mountain with the tablets. In the Bible, Moses shatters the tablets when he beholds the Israelites much later, cavorting around the Calf. Not so for Schoenberg. He has Moses shattering the tablets when Aaron reminds him that the tablets, too, are concrete images of the Torah Moses learned on Sinai. Even Moses needed an image.

With this, the opera comes quickly to an end. Moses is utterly defeated; his last words are "O word, that word, that I lack." Moses realizes that he will never find the words to convey what God means to him, that this dilemma is intractable, and that he has effectively failed.

Why the composer never completed the scoring of the opera is hotly debated. At the end of the brief, unscored third act, Aaron is killed, presumably by God. That would have been one possible resolution of the conflict; it would have expressed Schoenberg's conclusion that Moses really won out at the end. But Schoenberg never scored that act. We are left with the plaintive cry of a defeated Moses; there simply are no words.

We, too, are left with this tension. God is unimaginable; yet we need visual, intellectual, and linguistic representations of this God. Our ancestors never worshiped the sanctuary or the Temple. They understood it as a gateway to God. The cardinal sin is to worship our images as if they were the real thing. Then we, too, would be building golden calves.

Two Solitudes

DESPITE AN AVERSION TO COUNTING, particularly to counting people, we Jews do a great deal of counting in the course of our liturgical year.

We observe the Ten Days of Repentance between Rosh HaShanah and Yom Kippur. Mourners sit for the seven days of shivah and observe a more attenuated mourning period of thirty days or twelve months. We count seven weeks between Pesach and Shavuot.

We also count ten Jews to know whether we have a minyan, though here, we customarily recite a ten-word biblical verse, assigning one word to each Jew. We do the same in counting the seven times we wrap the *tefillin* strap around our arms. But in calling people up to the Torah reading, we identify them (at least after the first two) by number as the third aliyah, fourth aliyah, and so forth.

And then, of course, we proclaim God as *Echad*, One. This proclamation of the first verse of the Shema, in Deuteronomy 6:4, is undoubtedly the single most often recited passage in our entire liturgical tradition. Even those Jews who sit staring blankly throughout the service will come to life when the Torah is removed from the ark, to join in chanting this verse.

But surely proclaiming God as *Echad* is not a matter of counting. The classical translation of that word or phrase is "the Lord is One." But we also know that translation is ambiguous.

Maimonides seems to retain that sense of the Hebrew when he describes God (in his *Mishneh Torah*) as "one in every aspect from every angle, and in all ways in which unity is conceived. Hence the conclusion that God is the one who knows, is known, and is the knowledge (of God)—all these being one." But if God is "One" in this sense, then God is absolutely unique, which coincides with most modern translations of *Adonai Echad* as "the Lord alone."

The implication of that translation is that God alone is God, that there are no other gods like ours. The statement is not a mathematical claim but rather a statement about the nature of the biblical God, about God's absolute transcendence over all of creation and over all other so-called gods. The sense of the biblical verse, then, is that "the Lord our God alone is Lord," or "is the only Lord," or "is uniquely the Lord."

One of the more suggestive stretchings of that translation is proposed by Dr. Sherry Blumberg, who draws on her own personal experiences of being alone, and identifies God's aloneness with God's loneliness.

God? Lonely? Absolutely, if we take the biblical narrative seriously. If not, why create a world? Why create human beings? Why enter into a covenant or send prophets? All, it should be added, with singularly little success. It was the philosophical tradition that portrayed God as having it all together. In the Bible, God is portrayed as vulnerable, frustrated, and perpetually unsuccessful, yet consumed by infinite yearning and hope. It is precisely because of God's loneliness that the Bible portrays God as perpetually "in search of man," to quote Rabbi Abraham Joshua Heschel.

But there is one further use of the term *echad* in the Bible (I Chron. 17:21) that, not unexpectedly, the Talmudic Rabbis notice and that the Jewish Publication Society translates properly as "And who is like Your people Israel, a unique *(echad)* nation on earth."

In a flight of fantasy, the Rabbis portray God as wearing *tefillin* (Babylonian Talmud *Brachot* 6a). But what is inscribed in God's *tefillin?* Obviously, a phrase that corresponds to what is inscribed in our *tefillin.* If our *tefillin* contain the Shema, the phrase that portrays God as unique, then clearly God's *tefillin* must contain the phrase that portrays Israel as unique, this verse from First Chronicles.

So both God and Israel are unique, God among the gods, and Israel among the nations. And if both are unique, both are "alone" and both are lonely. That is the subtext of God's relationship with Israel. These two solitudes meet, engage each other, and understand each other precisely because both know what it means to be lonely. This verse, then, that most of us recite almost mindlessly, reflects a subtle theological claim.

Could that be why when we recite the Shema we customarily cover our eyes? Could this be a way to help us focus our attention on the deeper meaning of the words that we are saying at that moment?

God Is Moved

WITH THE OPENING VERSES OF THE BOOK of Exodus, the entire tone of the biblical narrative takes on a different character. No longer are singular individuals—the patriarchs, the matriarchs, and Joseph—at the heart of the story. The first verse of the book tells us the names of the "sons of Israel" who came to Egypt. But six verses later, it is "the Israelites" who were fertile and prolific, and in the very next verse, the new king of Egypt talks of "the Israelite people" who are too numerous and who have to be dealt with shrewdly.

Though the striking figure of Moses quickly emerges as the central figure of the narrative, essentially from here on in the Bible will be telling the story of the Israelite people. But not only does the human cast change; so too does the image of God. The most dramatic indication of that is reflected in three verses that are among the most powerful in all of scripture.

"A long time after that, the king of Egypt died. The Israelites were groaning under the bondage and cried out; and their cry for help from the bondage rose up to God. God heard their moaning, and God remembered God's covenant with Abraham and Isaac and Jacob. God looked upon the Israelites, and God took notice of them" (Ex. 2:23–25).

I encounter these three verses each year with renewed awe. What I sense here is a figure of great majesty, power, and determination. But God's majesty, power, and determination are generated by profound identification and compassion. This is a God who takes note of and is moved by the suffering of God's people. This mix of power and compassion is at the heart of the biblical image of God.

The power and the majesty we understand. But it is the compassion that troubles some of us. We have all been raised and educated in a system of thought that originated in Greece and that stems from the Western philosophical tradition that views God as beyond emotion. The notion of a God that can be "moved"—in both the literal and the figurative sense—was offensive to the Greek mind. It implied a lack or an insufficiency in God. If anything, God was the "prime mover," the "unmoved mover." God was what God was, eternal and unchanging. God was reason, knowledge, mind. To ascribe feelings to God was to demean God. But that Greek view of God was itself a projection of the Hellenistic system of values, and it is totally at odds with the biblical value system. The biblical mind-set could project feelings onto God precisely because it valued human emotion.

Rabbi Abraham Joshua Heschel, whose view of what he calls "God's pathos" is the central theme of his study of prophecy and later becomes the heart of his theological writings, poses the issue quite sharply: "Is it more compatible with our conception of the grandeur of God to claim that He is emotionally blind to the misery of man rather than profoundly moved? ... To the biblical mind, the conception of God as cold, detached, and unemotional is totally alien." For Rabbi Heschel, God was the most moved mover: "We tend to accept the Greek view of a God who has it all together, who represents self-enclosed perfection, as more sophisticated than the more primitive biblical image of an emotional God."

What is it in us that makes us suspect the biblical image? Above all, what does this tell us about the legitimacy of our own feelings? The biblical God cares. God cares about widows and orphans, the persecuted and the oppressed everywhere. And God cares about the Israelites suffering under bondage in Israel. It is God's emotion-laden concern for their fate, together with God's determination to keep the promises God made to our fore-fathers, that prompts their redemption. That's why we, too, are commanded to care.

But then, of course, another issue emerges. Why the slavery? Why the suffering in the first place? Why 430 years in Egypt (Ex. 12:40)? This is the question that in one form or another haunts the life experience of every believer. It is even more challenging for one who accepts the biblical image of God over the Greek philosophical image.

There is no biblical justification for this suffering. But the midrash offers, if not a justification, then at least a hint of con-solation. It notes that the text uses different forms of the same word—the Hebrew term *levenah*—to characterize both the bricks that the Israelites were forced to make in Egypt and the pave-ment that lay under the feet of God when Moses, Aaron, Nadab, Abihu, and the seventy elders of Israel "saw the God of Israel" at the climax of the Sinai event (Ex. 24:9–11).

The use of the same word suggests that God created God's own domain out of the bricks that the Israelites were forced to make in slavery. This is a statement of God's identification with the suffering of the people of Israel. God too, then, accompanied the Israelites into bondage, as God accompanied our people into exile and throughout our wanderings, and even into the Holocaust.

God suffers with our suffering. Beyond this, we are con-stantly reminded that we are to remember our experience of slavery and thus to strive to create a social structure that will not tolerate any form of oppression. Suffering provided the indispensable educational experience for a people who, like its God, is commanded to care deeply about people and their fate.

El Elyon

NEAR THE CONCLUSION OF THE STORY of the war of the four
kings against the five (Gen. 14:18–20), we find the enigmatic Melchizedek episode. Melchizedek is identified as king of
Salem and, more important, as a priest of *El Elyon*, "God Most
High." He blesses Abram in the name of *El Elyon* and further
identifies this deity as *Koneh shamayim va-aretz*, "Creator of
heaven and earth." In his later exchange with the king of Sodom
(Gen. 14:22), Abram repeats these two names and further identifies these names with the holy four-letter name of God.

In his excursus on *El Elyon* in the Jewish Publication Society
Commentary to Genesis (Excursus 7), Professor Nahum Sarna
notes that in extrabiblical sources, *El* and *Elyon* were two distinct
pagan deities. In our narrative, the Torah combines them into
one deity and identifies this conflated deity with first the One
God and then the One God who is also "creator of heaven and
earth."

The next step in the saga of this complex phrase is even more
fascinating. The entire appellation is transposed into the most

prominent place in our liturgy, the opening words of the opening benediction of the Amidah, which we recite at least three times daily, every day of the year.

In the Amidah, we begin with praise of "the Lord our God, the God of our ancestors, God of Abraham, God of Isaac, and God of Jacob" (and in some congregations, of Sarah, Rebecca, Leah, and Rachel as well). The text continues: "Great, mighty, and awesome God," and then our phrase, *El Elyon*, "God Most High."

Our liturgist was faced with an awesome challenge. We must begin the Amidah, he clearly felt, with a recitation of the attributes of this God to whom we are praying. But how is it even possible for humans to find the proper words to characterize this God? His solution was to go back to the characterizations that the Torah itself uses. That God is "great, mighty, and awesome" he found in Deuteronomy 10:17. That God is *El Elyon* he found in Genesis 14:19 in the words of the pagan priest Melchizedek.

The Babylonian Talmud (*Megillah* 25a) preserves an allusion to the dilemma of finding adequate words to characterize God in prayer. A prayer leader, in the presence of Rabbi Hanina, began by saying: "The great, the mighty, the awesome, the majestic, the strong, the powerful God." To which Rabbi Hanina responded: "Have you finished the praises of your Master? We would not recite even the first three had not Moses recorded them in the Torah [Deut. 10:17, cited above]. It is as if a man had thousands and thousands of gold dinars, and people praise his wealth by saying that he had a thousand. Would that not be an insult to him?"

In short, no human words can even begin to characterize our transcendent God—but we must say something. On this issue, then, minimalism is the rule. We use the words that the Torah uses, and in this case we even incorporate the words of a pagan priest, probably because Abram himself appropriates those very words.

Our appropriation of Melchizedek's formula, then, proceeded in two stages. The first, in the Torah itself, involved identifying his pagan deities with the One God of Abram and Israel. In the later tradition, this step is justified by identifying Melchizedek as a righteous gentile who worshiped the God of Abram, and his city, "Shalem," with Jerusalem.

The second stage takes place when his formula is introduced into our liturgy and, thereby, into the consciousness of all Jews to this day. Whenever we recite the Amidah, then, we praise God in words first uttered by a pagan priest centuries ago.

Finally, Sarna notes, the Melchizedek episode is designed to transform what began as a chapter in the annals of ancient warfare into a religious statement. It is not military prowess that enabled Abram to triumph, but rather the power of his One God, the God of Israel.

An Emotional Roller Coaster

W HAT WE EXPERIENCE AS A NINE-DAY FESTIVAL, Sukkot through Shemini Atzeret and Simchat Torah, is not, strictly speaking, one festival. The last two days are a separate festival, literally "a festival of its own." That is why, during Kiddush on the two evenings of these "last" days, we repeat the Shehecheyanu blessing that we say on the first days of Sukkot and other holidays.

But despite this distinction, we experience the eight days as one festival, which accounts for the roller coaster of emotions that assail us throughout this week. Consider just a few of these feelings.

Deuteronomy 16:15 tells us that on Sukkot, we "shall have nothing but joy." Rabbi Irving Greenberg (in his *The Jewish Way: Living the Holidays*) refers to the celebration of the last day, Simchat Torah, as a "holy pandemonium." We recite the Hosha Na (literally, "Save, we pray!") for redemption. We pray for rain. We recite Kohelet (Ecclesiastes), arguably the most pessimistic book in scripture. We read about the death of Moses. We say Yizkor for those who died. The very sukkah in which we live for seven days is itself a symbol of fragility and vulnerability; its shade must exceed its sunlight.

Nevertheless, we also wave the fruits of our harvest and thank God for all of God's blessings. And to complicate this emotional texture still further, Hoshana Rabbah, the seventh and last day of Sukkot, has many of the trappings of the Days of Awe.

The texture of Shemini Atzeret is not clear from the Bible. The most suggestive interpretation of the word *atzeret* is "restrain" or "hold back." God is portrayed as reluctant to allow the Israelites to return to their homes after celebrating Sukkot in Jerusalem. So God holds them back: "Stay a little longer," God says. To use a contemporary metaphor, God is like a parent whose children have come home for *yom tov* and are now ready to go back to their homes again. But the parents are reluctant to have them leave, so they plead, "Stay a little longer," or "Take a later flight."

Shemini Atzeret remains an ambiguous holiday: It is its own day, and yet it is also intimately tied to Sukkot. The clearest expression of that ambiguity is the fact that all of the obvious symbols that we use to celebrate Sukkot disappear. We no longer sit in the sukkah; we no longer wave the *lulav* and *etrog*. Sukkot is extraordinarily rich in visual symbols, but they all disappear on Shemini Atzeret.

Rabbi Greenberg provides a striking explanation of this sudden disappearance: "The message is that all the rituals and symbolic language are important but ultimately they remain just symbols." The one word I would quarrel with in his sentence is "just," though I understand why the author uses it. The whole point of a symbol is that it should extend beyond itself. It should be transparent; that is, we should see through it to what it stands for. When a symbol becomes opaque, when it blocks instead of reveals, when it takes the place of what it points to, then it has failed in its purpose. To take a secular example, we do not worship the American flag. What we do acknowledge is the nation "for which it stands."

Shemini Atzeret denudes Sukkot of its visual and tactile symbols. We are left to our own resources, standing, so to speak, naked before God. We confront the complex messages of the season: human life is fragile and death is real, as are the many joys that come from God's bountiful blessings. What we have called the festival's emotional roller coaster is nothing less than the roller coaster intrinsic to human life.

And if we look at the holiday season as a whole, we begin with the Days of Awe and end with rejoicing over Torah. Once we have traversed the emotional terrain from awe to joy, we can now return to our daily lives. The concluding words of the Shemini Atzeret haftarah seem to be quite appropriate now. After Solomon finished consecrating his Temple, we are told that "he let the people go. They bade the king good-bye and went to their homes, joyful and glad of heart over all the goodness that the Lord had shown to God's servant David and God's people Israel" (I Kings 8:66).

The Ambiguities
of a Metaphor

T O SAY ANYTHING ABOUT THE NATURE OF GOD is to resort to
the language of metaphor. But the problem with using
metaphors to speak of God is that the same metaphor evokes different responses from different people.

Take the familiar metaphor that God is our shepherd. It
appears everywhere in the Bible and in our liturgy, most notably
at the opening of Psalm 23, arguably the best known of all the
psalms. "The Lord is my shepherd, I shall not want" is the most
familiar translation, though JPS translates "... I lack nothing."
The popularity of this psalm rests on the notion that it speaks of
God as the source of security and comfort. That God is our shepherd is a metaphorical way of saying that God nurtures and cares
for us. Hospital chaplains tell me that they are invariably asked
to recite this psalm at the bedside of a critically ill patient.

Imagine my surprise, then, when, as I was teaching this
psalm and referring to this conventional interpretation, a student reacted quite violently: "If God is a shepherd, then I am a
sheep. But I very much resent being referred to as a sheep! Sheep

are passive. I am not passive." I was very much taken by that reaction, and in support, I referred the class to Psalm 44, specifically to verses 12 and 23. The psalm as a whole is a bitter indictment of God for having abandoned Israel to its foes. Verse 12 reads, "You let them [our enemies] devour us like sheep; You disperse us among the nations." And verse 23, arguably the bleakest passage in the entire *Tanakh*, reads: "It is for Your sake that we are slain all day long, that we are regarded as sheep to be slaughtered." What kind of a shepherd is this who allows his flock to be slaughtered, and ironically, slaughtered for his own sake?

A more ambiguous use of the same metaphor occurs at the climax of the High Holy Days Musaf liturgy in the Unetaneh Tokef *piyut*. There the metaphor compares God's judging us at this season to a shepherd reviewing his flock: "As a shepherd musters his sheep, and passes them beneath his staff, do You pass and record, count and visit every living thing, appointing the measure of every creature's life and decreeing its destiny." Not as harsh a use of the metaphor as in Psalm 44, but hardly an expression of a nurturing and comforting God.

The metaphor also appears in *Parashat Pinchas*, in a passage that has always touched me. God informs Moses that he will not be permitted to bring Israel into the Promised Land because of the incident over the hitting of the rock. He, too, will die in the wilderness. Moses does not utter a word of protest. Instead, in a passage that is quoted each year at the Jewish Theological Seminary as part of the ritual of ordination of a new class of rabbis, Moses asks God to appoint his successor: "Let the Lord, Source of the breath of all flesh, appoint someone over the community who shall go out before them and come in before them, and who shall take them out and bring them in, so that the Lord's community may not be like sheep that have no shepherd" (Num. 17:16–17). In response, God has Moses appoint Joshua as his successor.

I confess that for about fifty years, now, I have heard this passage recited at each year's rabbinic ordination ceremony, without really paying attention to its multilayered message. On a superficial level, do the laypeople in attendance (and congregational search committees and boards) view themselves as sheep to be herded by their shepherd-rabbis? My sense is that if anything, they would echo my student who was deeply offended by the notion that she was a sheep. No sense of passiveness there!

On a more ironic level, what kind of message was Moses delivering to God? Isn't God Israel's shepherd? Isn't God supposed to take care of Israel? Why, then, do they need a human shepherd? Is this possibly Moses' subtle protest, his way of saying to God, "With You, God, as shepherd, maybe we do need a human shepherd as well!"

Finally, in this post-Holocaust era, when the metaphor of "like sheep to the slaughter" appears everywhere in Holocaust literature, should we not have a new appreciation for the ambiguity of this metaphor, and possibly of all theological metaphors?

To all of this, many are tempted to react, "But it's only a metaphor!" The proper response to that is, "Never say 'only' a metaphor, but rather 'nothing less' than a metaphor." For when speaking of God, metaphors are all we have. The only issue is "which" metaphor, and that is arguably the most complex theological issue we face.

A Single Sacred Spot

A COUPLE I KNOW MARK THEIR WEDDING ANNIVERSARY by returning every year to the restaurant they went to on their first date. They sit at that very same table and spend the evening reminiscing about the history of their relationship, their life together, its ups and its downs, and what lies ahead for them. They could do this anywhere, of course, but for them, this particular place serves to generate a flood of memories, feelings, and associations. It has a privileged status for them.

On a broader scale, Americans do the same thing. We return to the Statue of Liberty, to Ellis Island, to the burial ground at Gettysburg, or to the Lincoln Memorial. Approach the Lincoln Memorial, walk into the space enclosed by the columns, and stand in front of that statue—a host of feelings and associations engulf you as to what America is all about. You feel differently, act differently, than you do in the surrounding streets.

And then there is sacred space. Every religion singles out a spot on earth that constitutes the central point of reference around which the rest of the community's world is organized. It is usually the spot where God first appeared to the community's ancestors. That is why it is often portrayed as a gateway, an opening through which symbolically God descended to earth and human beings ascended to heaven.

The Bible preserves a number of references to such sacred places. Moriah, that spot where Abraham was prepared to sacrifice his son, is referred to as the mountain where God is to be perceived (Gen. 22:14). Later, in Exodus, there is the burning bush and ultimately Sinai itself.

The story of Jacob's ladder (Gen. 28:10–19) is a classic example of how a single spot on earth became sacred to our community. On his way to Haran, Jacob stops for the night and has a dream. The symbolism of the dream—a ladder set on the ground with its top reaching into heaven, and angels ascending and descending—captures the sense of a gateway that unites heaven and earth. Jacob awakes and clearly perceives the meaning of his dream: "Surely the Lord is present in this place.... This is none other than the abode of God, and that is the gateway to heaven." To commemorate the experience, Jacob sets up the stone on which he rested as a pillar, anoints it with oil, and names the site Beth El, the House of God.

The various sacred spaces recorded in the Bible have had a mixed history. The most curious of all is Sinai. We might have expected that Sinai would become the central sacred place for Jews, yet it never did. Apart from the revelation recorded in Exodus and recalled in Deuteronomy and again in Nehemiah, Sinai is just about forgotten in the rest of the Bible. There is no record of any shrine, any memorial, or any act of worship connected with Sinai. We don't even know precisely where Sinai is.

But Moriah, site of the *Akedah*, is a very different matter. That spot is identified in II Chronicles 3:1 as the place where the Temple in Jerusalem was to be built. The Temple itself was a later version of the desert sanctuary that in early Israelite history was the axis around which the Jewish religious world was structured.

It was the gateway to heaven, for at the heart of the Temple stood the ark. On the ark's cover were two cherubim with their wings arching over their heads, and the space between the wings of the cherubim was the spot through which God appeared to the community. Numbers 7:89 records that the heavenly voice spoke to Moses from above the cover that was on top of the ark "between the two cherubim."

But what about Beth El? Here the midrash comes to the rescue (see Rashi on Gen. 28:17). Drawing on the symbolism of this giant ladder, the midrash explains that the foot of this ladder stood in the southernmost part of Be'er Sheva, and its head in the northernmost part of Beth El. Its very center, then, stood precisely over Moriah/Jerusalem.

Effectively, then, the midrash conflates Beth El and Moriah so that they become one spot. And Jerusalem/Beth El/Moriah became the center of the Jewish religious world. It was the site of the Temple, for centuries the only place where God could be worshiped. It was the site of pilgrimages. To this day, even after the destruction of the Temple, whenever Jews stand to worship, we face Jerusalem.

But with all that, in our day things have changed significantly. We acknowledge the religious centrality of Jerusalem in many symbolic ways, but we also build synagogues wherever we wish to build them on any spot on earth. When ten Jews enter a building or synagogue room containing a Torah scroll and worship God, that spot becomes the center of that community's religious world, the spot where we encounter God.

For us today, no single space is inherently sacred. In fact, space is no longer sanctified by God. We ourselves sanctify a space by deciding to worship there. We are convinced that wherever it is that we choose to worship, God is accessible to us, as accessible as God was to our ancestors in Jerusalem. We have revived an entirely different model of sacred space, also preserved in the Bible, which teaches that our ancestors in the course of their desert wanderings could erect their sanctuary anywhere in that wilderness. True, it was God who told them where to do so. But that was never limited to one inherently sacred place.

What destroyed the model of one inherent gateway to heaven was the notion of the monotheistic God. If God is truly God, then God can be reached from any place on earth.

Wherever it is, then, that we turn to God in prayer, that spot becomes our Beth El. For us, as for our ancestor Jacob, we too stand at the gateway to heaven in the abode of God, and we too can dream of a ladder with its foot on earth and its top reaching to the heavens.

When Liturgy Is Problematic

WHAT DO WE DO WITH A PRAYER when we may no longer believe what it says? Such a passage can be found in Deuteronomy 11:13–21, one that also plays a central role in Jewish religious life. It begins with the words *Vehaya im shamo'a* ("If, then, you obey the commandments") and proceeds to instruct us to bind these words as a sign on our hands and as frontlets (or symbols) on our foreheads, and to inscribe them on the doorposts of our houses and on our gates. Because the rabbinic interpretation of "these words" is literally these very words, this passage became one of the biblical passages that are transcribed onto parchment and inserted into our *tefillin* and mezuzot.

The passage also instructs us to recite these words "when you lie down and when you get up." Again, the Rabbis took this instruction literally, and this entire passage became the second of the three (together with Deut. 6:4–9, and Num. 15:37–41) that we recite twice a day as *K'riat Sh'ma*, the recitation of the Shema, the heart of our morning and evening service.

As far back as we know, these three paragraphs were recited as part of formal Jewish worship. (See, for example, *Mishnah Tamid* 5:1, which seems to reflect the practice in the days of the Second Temple.) Its daily recitation, then, is as ancient a practice as we have.

Whatever its content, that our loyalty to God's commands will be rewarded by rainfall and natural plenty, and our flaunting of God's will by drought and famine, became problematic to some modern Jews. The paragraph was dropped from early American versions of the Reform liturgy and, in 1945, Mordecai Kaplan also eliminated it from his Reconstructionist siddur with the comment "that the very rainfall is influenced by human conduct, we know, is not true."

That last claim makes fascinating reading today, when our new ecological consciousness has taught us that there is indeed a very close relationship between human behavior and our environment. It's not surprising then that this passage has returned in the latest edition of the Reconstructionist prayer book.

Troubling prayers can be handled in different ways. We can simply eliminate them from the prayer book, or eliminate or change their more problematic words. Or we can add other options for those who find they simply cannot recite the traditional passage. Or, finally, we can retain the original Hebrew intact, and either use the translation to interpret the passage in a less literal manner, or rely on the text's ability to yield multiple theological interpretations.

By and large, Kaplan and the early Reformers resorted to the first two strategies. That's what makes their prayer books so discordant to traditionalist ears. But that strategy is not a modern invention. We know, for example, that if some of the medieval Jewish sages had their way, Kol Nidrei, surely as sacred a prayer as we have, would have been eliminated long ago.

But the editors of the new Reconstructionist prayer book seem to have largely abandoned Kaplan's strategy and relied more on the alternatives. In fact, what makes it possible for them to reintroduce the passage is precisely that they interpret it in a radically modern way.

As a good Conservative Jew, liturgical change is a source of unending tension for me. My colleagues on the Jewish religious left have made and continue to make many radical changes in the prayer book, and my colleagues on my religious right are leery of even the slightest change. I, and I believe most of my Conservative colleagues, agonize over each one.

My basic impulse is to be conservative (this time with a lower-case "c") on liturgical change, however liberal I may be theologically. My sense is that there has to be a record of classical Jewish thinking on the basic issues of Jewish belief. After the canonization of the Bible, that place is the core portions of our liturgy. In fact, I use the prayer book as my text for teaching rabbinic theology. I may not agree with everything my ancestors recited. I then can choose not to recite a passage at any one service, or to struggle with it, or to substitute an alternative. But we should not cavalierly change the prayer book itself.

My basic quarrel with those who do is that they deprive future generations of the opportunity to learn about classical Jewish thought and then to do what the editors had to do, to conduct their own personal struggle with those beliefs as articulated in the prayer.

At the same time, I am painfully aware of the fact that for many of my contemporaries, the traditional liturgy is simply a barrier to genuine prayer. I am also aware that our liturgy has always been in the process of change.

So I remain in a state of acute tension about each of these changes. I have gradually become more comfortable with including the matriarchs in the first benediction of the Amidah. However, I refuse to change the phrase praising God "Who resurrects the dead" to "Source of life" in the second benediction, as in the Reform and Reconstructionist prayer books, because I believe

that the original is profoundly true and that the change trivial-
izes a core doctrine of our tradition. I also struggle constantly
and without a clear resolution with gender issues in the liturgy,
particularly with its characterizations of God.

Are there any general guidelines for us to follow? Very few.
First, we should retain a classical text until we are convinced of
its inadequacy. Second, it is always easier to add than to eliminate. Third, we should experiment with new formulations in living liturgical situations before putting them into printed prayer
books, where they tend to become immutable. Finally, only a
worshipping community can render judgment on a liturgical
text; editors and editorial committees should always work
within a praying community before publishing their texts.
Finally, we must learn to live with the inevitable tensions that
accompany a nonliteralist approach to Judaism.

That final issue is probably the most important and the most
difficult. We intuitively look at religion as one of those settings,
increasingly rare in the modern world, where we can find a sense
of peace. But paradoxically, it is precisely the richness of the traditional liturgy and our wish to take its content seriously that
generate the tensions we feel when we open the prayer book.
Desirable or not, we must learn to live with that tension.

Selective Memories

THE MOST STRIKING LITURGICAL THEME in the generally enigmatic festival of Rosh HaShanah is memory. The festival itself is identified as Yom HaZikaron, literally "the Memory Day," the day in which we celebrate the power of memory.

Whose memory? Ostensibly God's. We jog God's memory. We pray that God remember the loyalty of the patriarchs, Abraham's readiness to sacrifice his son, and the covenant with Noah and later with our ancestors at Sinai, and, in return, that God grant us life and a year of blessing. But why do we need to remind God of all this? Why indeed? For one of the most notable of the images of God in this festival's liturgy is that God remembers everything. On two occasions, God is referred to as *Zocher kol hanishkachot*, literally as "remembering all that is forgotten."

The Zichronot (or "Memories") prayer, one of the three units added to this day's Musaf service, begins with a more expanded version of that image: "You remember everything that was done from eternity, all that You created from of old. Before You, all that is hidden, all that was concealed from the beginning of time, is revealed. Before Your glorious throne, nothing is forgotten; nothing is hidden from Your eyes."

If so, why does God need reminding? Because sometimes God's memory, like our own, goes astray. That Zichronot passage includes ten biblical passages in which God is described as remembering something. One is Jeremiah 2:2: "Go proclaim to Jerusalem," God tells the prophet. "I remember to your favor the devotion of your youth, your love as a bride, how you followed Me in the wilderness, in a land not sown."

That is an astonishing example of a distorted memory. God remembers the years of Israel's wandering in the desert following the Exodus as a period of Israel's devotion to God, as a honeymoon period. Yet if we read the historical record of that period as described in the Torah, it was hardly a honeymoon. The very opposite! Those years were marked by constant discord, rebellion, wrangling, complaining, and frustration on both sides. Indeed, that desert generation so angered God that it was condemned to die in the wilderness. Only their children would enter the Promised Land. Hardly an instance of devotion!

But God forgets nothing, we are told in the liturgy. Apparently, sometimes God does forget some things, or chooses to forget, or decides to forget, as do we. Apparently, God's memory, like ours, is selective.

We have to remember that everything we say about God is taken from our own human experience. We human beings know nothing objectively about God's nature. That's because God is God and we are human beings. Yet we are driven to speak of God. So we take our common human experience, of which we know a great deal, and project it onto God.

In this instance, we begin with our own experience of memory. We are acutely aware that it is memory that confers identity. Our memory ties together our entire life experience, makes it uniquely ours, makes us what we are distinctively. Our communal memory does the same with our identity as a people. We are never more acutely aware of the power of memory than when we lose that power, when we watch our dear ones whose memory is disabled gradually lose their sense of who they are.

We are aware that sometimes, more frequently the older we get, our memory fails us, or distorts the past, so that we are no longer as certain as we should be that events really happened just as we recall them. We tend to view this as our failure, so that when we talk about God—who, of course, is perfect—we insist that God, at least, remembers everything, just as it happened.

We also know that sometimes to forget is a blessing. When we recall our early years as parents of young children, or the early years of our marriages, our memories become selective. Nostalgia sets in. We romanticize those years. We choose, or decide, to forget the rough spots.

That is why on this Rosh HaShanah festival, we need to tell God precisely what it is we want God to remember. What we are jogging is not God's memory overall but rather the selective dimension of God's memories. We want God to forget some things—the rough spots—and to remember only the golden years.

There is a delightful irony to the liturgist's including Jeremiah 2:2 in the list of God's memories. He knew full well that the verse distorts what really happened in those desert years. That's precisely why he put it there. Indeed, the entire list is selective; it deals only with the happy memories. The last thing we need, on this day above all, is for God to recall the problematic ones.

PART III

Revelation and Law

Narrative and Law

*P*ARASHAT *MISHPATIM* BEGINS WITH LAWS about Hebrew slaves and concludes with the most enigmatic mystical experience in the entire Torah. Simply put, it begins with law and ends with theology.

Mishpatim consists of four chapters, Exodus 21–24. The initial three, preceded by the Ten Commandments in Exodus 20, are a code of law, the first systematic code addressed to the Israelites in the Torah, what scholars have called the Covenant Code because it is embedded in the narrative of the revelation of God's covenant with Israel at Sinai.

The code itself lacks any apparent order. It deals with civil, criminal, and ritual laws, from homicide to goring oxen to usury to the Sabbath to the dietary laws, with judicial procedures and moral exhortations all assembled together.

What these laws all share is the assumption that Israel's social life demands structure. These structures are articulated in the language of law. There is a right way of behaving and a wrong way, dos and don'ts, positive commands and negative commands.

And all of them are called by the generic term *mishpatim*, "rules," or, more generally, legal enactments. The author of the laws is God. It is God who commands how Israel is to behave.

Law is an expression of covenant. Both are jurisprudential institutions. No single issue did more to shape all of Judaism to this very day than the fact that law originated in covenant; covenant generated law. From then on, the most characteristically Jewish form of religious expression is law. We call it halachah.

But halachah is embedded in a story. The story begins with the creation of the world, continues with the patriarchs and Joseph, the descent to Egypt, and the redemption from slavery, and concludes with the revelation at Sinai. It continues later with the building of the desert sanctuary, the trek through the wilderness, and the conquest of the Promised Land, through exile and redemption and the rest. We call this story aggadah. Halachah is embedded in aggadah. Law is embedded in theology. The broader framework, then, is aggadah, halachah, aggadah or, in our modern idiom, theology, halachah, theology.

When we claim that halachah is "embedded" in aggadah, we are using a thoroughly appropriate metaphor. Law is surrounded by story. Halachah may well be the most characteristically Jewish form of religious expression, but it is aggadah, theology, that lends it authority. Without the story, we would have no idea why there is halachah in the first place. Why does God care enough to structure our communal life? to reveal codes of law? How did the law get to us? Why is it authoritative? These questions underlie Jewish law and are all pure theology.

The code ends with chapter 23. In the parashah's concluding chapter, chapter 24, Moses repeats the laws to the people, who commit themselves to observing them; he writes down the commands (Judaism eternally centers itself around a book), erects an altar, and solemnizes the covenant with ritual sacrifice.

These events should serve as the climax of this chapter in the story, but they don't. What follows is that enigmatic mystical experience. Moses, Aaron and his sons, and seventy elders ascend the mountain, "and they saw the God of Israel: under God's feet there was the likeness of a pavement of sapphire, like the very sky for purity. Yet God did not raise God's hand against the leaders of the Israelites; they beheld God, and they ate and drank" (Ex. 24:10–11).

They saw God? They ate and drank? And they were not damaged? Just like that? But no human being can see God and live, we are told later in this book. And if we were privileged to see God, would we eat and drink? Why is this part of the story told so matter-of-factly, as if it were the most natural, everyday experience possible? What does it all mean?

Nothing in the text helps answer any of these questions. But what amazes me is the inclusion of this episode in a parashah that is all law. The parashah could have ended with chapter 23, and we wouldn't have to deal with the contrast in such an immediate way. But no. The parashah is all halachah, and then, as if to remind us that Judaism is much more than law, we are handed this prototypical piece of theology, a classic mystical experience, and a new set of questions that are pure theology.

This theologian is reassured.

Sinai Was a Moment

EXODUS 19, ARGUABLY THE FOUNDATION for the Jewish religion as a whole, provides the setting for God's revelation of Torah to Israel. Each time I read that narrative, I have a growing sense of its inherently mysterious quality. My impulse as an academician is to try to penetrate the mystery, to "comprehend" it conceptually, to "explain" it to my students. But the narrative resists my every attempt. It is as if the cloud that enveloped the mountain serves also to shroud the narrative. What really happened at Sinai?

I then recall what Rabbi Abraham Joshua Heschel wrote about this chapter. He counsels us against trying to "understand" the biblical account of the revelation at Sinai. It was never intended to be a literally accurate description of an event, he claims, but rather a song—a celebration, not a photograph. And then that unforgettable sentence in *God in Search of Man*: "As a report about revelation the Bible itself is a midrash."

Imagine, then, if that chapter were written as a poem, just as Moses' "Song at the Sea" in Exodus 15 is written in the Torah scroll. In that latter passage, it is obvious that we are dealing with poetry, not prose. The opening verse itself tells us that this is a song, not a straightforward narrative. When it tells us the waters of the sea "stood straight like a wall," we realize that we are dealing with the language of metaphor. We don't need to understand it literally. We shouldn't even *try* to understand it literally.

But Exodus 19 is not supposed to be a song. At least it would seem that the Bible itself understands it as a historical narrative, as prose, not poetry. What happens when we read it as poetry, as a complex of metaphors? Does God literally "come down" on the mountain? Is God literally in space, "up" rather than "down"? Does God literally "speak"? Were there literal shofar blasts? thunder and lightning? and dense cloud upon the mountain? Or are all of these poetic touches designed, as Heschel suggests, to enhance and celebrate the mystery?

Does it make a difference how we understand Exodus 19?

Very much so. How we relate to Judaism does not rest on how we understand the "Song at the Sea," but it does depend on how we understand Sinai. Sinai is about the covenant, about the authority of Torah and of halachah. Those of us who read this chapter as a literal description of a historical event base our understanding of Judaism on the fact that God did literally speak at Sinai, that the Torah is literally God's word and therefore is binding on all Jews, forever and unchanging, from generation to generation.

In contrast, those of us who read the chapter as a song or as a midrash acknowledge that what we have is a human response to, or an interpretation of, an event that surpasses human understanding and language. That's precisely what we mean by midrash: a human interpretation of a text, or here, of an event.

That way of reading the story of Sinai introduces the human factor into Torah from the very outset. Or, as Heschel continues, the two terms for what happened at Sinai are *mattan Torah* and *kabbalat Torah,* God's "giving of the Torah" and Israel's "accepting of the Torah." What God transmitted had to be formulated in human terms.

"The act of revelation is a mystery," Heschel writes, "while the record of revelation is a literary fact, phrased in the language of man." That's why Exodus 19 is a song or a midrash. He adds, "It was a moment in which God was not alone."

This way of understanding Exodus 19 transforms the broader issue of the authority of Torah in a way that many of our contemporaries can only welcome. If, from the outset, Torah was embodied in human terms, then all subsequent generations of Jews have the right and the responsibility to acknowledge that same human factor in how they read the mandate of Torah, in the light of their own specific historical and cultural contexts. We, then, can do the same for our own day.

I leave the last word on this issue to one of my students. Reflecting on the fact that to this day, no one knows for sure precisely where Mount Sinai is located, he echoed Heschel in suggesting we understand Sinai not as a place but as a moment—a moment when God was not alone, a moment when God and Israel entered into a relationship.

Boundaries

BOUNDARIES ARE IMPORTANT. That is the theme of the concluding verses of Leviticus 11. They provide a concluding statement of purpose for the list of forbidden foods outlined in this chapter. Read this in conjunction with a parallel passage in Leviticus 20:22–26 that follows the list of forbidden sexual relations. Together, they speak to us of the importance of boundaries.

In Leviticus 11, the central command is that we are to be holy (from the Hebrew *kadosh*) as (or "because") God is holy. How are we to do this? One way is by "distinguishing [*lehavdil*] between the unclean and the clean, between the living things that may be eaten and the living things that may not be eaten" (Lev. 11:47). In Leviticus 20:25–26, in place of "distinguish," the Jewish Publication Society translation is "set apart." We should set apart the clean beasts from the unclean. Why? Again, because God is holy, and also because God has "set you apart from other peoples" (Lev. 20:26). But what does it mean to claim that God is *kadosh*?

"Holy," "distinguish," and "set apart" are all synonyms. The first thing we can learn from this usage, then, is to clarify the original intent of *kadosh,* or "holy," one of those terms—another is "spiritual"—I am wary of using because, through overuse, they have been robbed of their precise meaning.

Kadosh originally meant "set apart." Eventually it came to mean "special." "Distinguish" shares the same ambiguity. One can distinguish between two different kinds of people, for example, but we can also say that someone is distinguished; he is not only set apart but he is also special in some way.

The second lesson is the essential parallel between Kiddush and Havdalah, the rituals that open and close our celebration of Shabbat. Each is a "setting apart" ritual; each sets apart Shabbat from the common days that precede and follow it. The Friday night liturgy describes God as being *mekadesh;* the Saturday night liturgy uses the synonym *hamavdil.* In both cases, this set-apart day becomes distinguished, in the "special" sense of the term.

We also learn that to say that Israel is an *am kadosh* is to say that we are to be a set-apart people, distinguished from the other nations of the earth. By extension this leads to the notion of a "chosen" or "special" people. Finally, we are to be set apart because God, too, is set apart—from other so-called gods.

The Torah as a whole, then, articulates a broad pattern of "set apartedness," distinctions in time and space (for Israel is also a holy land), among peoples, and in how we live our lives (for example, in what we eat and don't eat, in our sexual relationships, and in life-cycle events) that ultimately bear upon God as well. All of these distinctions underlie and support one another. In each case, some ritual is introduced that marks the boundary between one and the next.

The grand purpose of Torah, then, is to infuse our consciousness with boundaries, or distinctions. In a word, the purpose of the whole is to create structures. Structures provide a sense of order or cosmos. They shield us from the anarchy or chaos that are so much a part of our daily experience. Halachah, the pattern of Jewish law, is one grand ordering device.

People cope with disorder in different ways. Some people thrive on it; others don't. Some of us are constantly ordering the papers on our desks into piles. We make lists of what we are to do today, what calls we are to return, what letters we are to answer. We keep meticulous appointment books. We live in constant anxiety that our lives may tumble out of control. Others seem to manage quite well without any of these devices.

But viewed from an anthropological or psychological point of view, religion seems to assume that all human beings need to feel that on the broadest possible canvas, their world is fundamentally ordered. Of course, chaos always threatens to overwhelm us, but then, our religious traditions give us the resources to reimpose order on the disorder. Think, for example, of the richness of our rituals for handling death and mourning.

Finally, a note on the mystifying incident involving Nadab and Abihu, the two sons of Aaron the High Priest who offered an "alien fire" before the Lord and were consumed (Lev. 10:1–3). Interpretations of this passage abound, but at its core, their offense seems to have been that they trivialized the sanctuary. That's the implication of the term "alien fire." Or, to use our terminology, they blurred the boundary between the sacred and the common.

We may not view these boundaries in as inflexible a way as the Torah does, or blurring them as cardinal an offense. But in this view, the incident underlines once again the primary message that boundaries are important.

Aggadah and Halachah

IF SOME RABBINIC AUTHORITIES had had their way, the Torah
would have begun not with Genesis but with Exodus 12.

That is the suggestion advanced by Rashi (quoting Rabbi
Yitzchak) in his commentary to the very first verse of the Bible:
"The Torah should have begun with the verse, 'This month shall
mark for you the beginning of the months; it shall be the first of
the months for you' (Ex. 12:2), for this is the first commandment
addressed to the entire people of Israel."

Of course, the suggestion is quickly rejected, and a reason-
able explanation is advanced for beginning the Torah with the
story of creation. But as is frequently the case, the question is
much better than the answer, and that the question should have
been asked in the first place is quite remarkable.

It is the implicit assumption underlying a question of this
kind that shocks: Torah, and by extension Jewish religion, is
essentially halachah, mitzvot or commandments, a body of laws;
anything that is not explicitly a matter of halachah does not
belong in the Torah. That is why the Torah should properly

begin with the first mitzvah addressed to the entire community. And that is why the entire book of Genesis and the first eleven chapters of Exodus (and, by extension, the remaining nonlegal portions of the Torah) do not belong in our sacred scriptures.

But if Judaism is essentially a matter of religious law, then what role does theology or the entire system of Jewish belief play in Jewish religious life? Typically, those Jews who agree with Rabbi Yitzchak would argue that from the outset, the authentic Jew was the Jew who obeyed God's commands, who followed God's ways and listened to God's voice. To this day, then, we should measure authentic Jewish commitment by observance of the mitzvot.

In contrast to this emphasis Judaism places on law, it has never put a premium on clearly defining the content of the Jewish belief system. Judaism has no dogmas, these authorities argue, at least nothing similar to what some forms of Christianity proclaim. The centerpiece of the Roman Catholic mass, for example, is the credo ("I believe") in which the Christian is asked to articulate the content of Christian belief. The Shema is frequently touted as the central article of Jewish belief, but it hardly approaches the range of content and the explicitness of the Christian credo.

In short, these Jews argue, don't worry too much about what you believe. Keep the mitzvot and you will be an authentic Jew.

Thankfully, the Torah does include the story of the creation of the world, the patriarchal narratives, and the story of the Exodus from Egypt before coming to the first mitzvah addressed to the entire community. And therein lies a message that every serious Jew must hearken to. It is simply impossible to accept the entire body of halachah incumbent on the Jew without a broader theological or ideological base that gives the system as a whole coherent meaning.

For the central question that the halachah itself cannot provide an answer to is, Why halachah? Not why Shabbat or why kashrut, but why halachah in the first place? Why is it that Judaism is so concerned with prescribed forms of behavior? What does it mean to speak of a God who commands? How do we understand the claim that God revealed these mitzvot? What happened at Sinai? Finally, why take any of it seriously?

It is precisely to answer those questions that the Torah begins where it does. There is a direct relation between a God who cares enough to create an ordered world and who created human beings with freedom, and a God who cares enough to liberate a people from captivity, enter into a covenant with them, and command them to create an ordered social structure.

It might have been possible in certain periods of Jewish history for Jews to bind themselves to the halachah without an underlying belief system to support that commitment. But then there were those other periods that produced, to take one example, a Maimonides who felt he had to write a major philosophical treatise precisely to justify allegiance to Jewish religion and its halachah.

If anything, our own age today is much closer to that of Maimonides. Once again, we Jews live in an open society. Once again, we are exposed to multiple competing ideologies. This, too, is an age of rampant individualism, of critical inquiry, of seductive secularisms and humanisms. It is an age where all authority systems are questioned.

This, then, is an age where the case for commitment to the halachah must be made. Halachah cannot simply justify itself. It is no longer sufficient to tell Jews simply to observe Shabbat and kashrut, and not to worry about what they are supposed to believe. In fact, it is precisely those Jews we most want to attract who will insist that they cannot simply act without understanding why they are acting this particular way.

It is hard to know how serious Rabbi Yitzchak or Rashi was in suggesting that Genesis and Exodus 1–11 don't belong in the Torah. But it is quite clear that many Jewish authorities in succeeding generations have been very serious in suggesting that theology is not a central form of Jewish religious expression. Those who share this belief might well ponder, then, why Exodus 12 occupies precisely the place it does in Torah literature.

The Best Interest of
Judaism Clause

I HAVE LONG BEEN FASCINATED by the "best interest of baseball"
clause, one of the more frequently invoked rules in Major
League Baseball. Briefly, that clause gives the commissioner of
Major League Baseball broad authority to legislate or render
decisions that, in his eyes, are in "the best interest of baseball."
Team owners and the players may or may not always agree with
the commissioner's decisions, in which case the owners can fire
him after his term has expired. But barring that, the rules of the
game grant the commissioner broad personal authority to shape
the culture of the sport.

What interests me here is first, the recognition that no body
of rules, however comprehensive, can cover every possible even-
tuality, and second, that the rules themselves grant someone the
authority to interpret them in whatever way he sees fit—with no
need to justify his decisions except for claiming that he is acting
"in the best interest of baseball" as he understands it.

A Jewish version of the "best interest of baseball" clause can
be found in Deuteronomy 17, where we are told that "if a case is

too baffling for you to decide ... you shall promptly repair to the place that the Lord your God will have chosen, and appear before the levitical priests, or the magistrate in charge at the time, and present your problem. When they have announced to you the verdict in the case, you shall carry out the verdict ... observing scrupulously all their instructions to you.... You must not deviate from the verdict that they announce to you either to the right or to the left" (Deut. 17:8–11).

This passage constitutes the Torah's realization that even its body of rules can never be comprehensive enough. It therefore empowers some future authority to rule or legislate as that authority sees fit. The later tradition acknowledges that power. We should never say, we are told, that the judges of bygone days were better than those of our day. All we have are our own authorities. "Jephtah in his generation is equal to Samuel in his" (Babylonian Talmud *Rosh HaShanah*, 25b).

This passage legitimatizes rabbinic authority for all future generations. We today praise God for having commanded us to light the Chanukah lights when, of course, there is no such command in the Torah. How can we do this? Maimonides replies that, in fact, we are praising God for having commanded us to obey the Rabbis who have the authority to legislate the lighting of Chanukah lights. Their command, whatever it may be, has God's explicit authority behind it. They can be said to be acting "in the best interest of Judaism."

However, on this issue, there is one major difference between baseball and Judaism. Baseball has only one set of major leagues and one commissioner, and the rules of the game are explicit as to how that commissioner is to be elected or deposed. In contrast, there are many Jewish communities and multiple rabbinic authorities. The divisiveness that is part of our communal life stems precisely from the fact that different portions of our community recognize different rabbinic authorities, that each of these mini-communities has different views on what makes for a rabbinic authority in the first place, and that these authorities have very different visions of how Torah should be interpreted in our day.

To take one example, the ongoing controversy regarding "who is a Jew" was hardly about that issue. It is, in fact, much more a question of "who is a rabbi," or which rabbinic authority rests behind the conversion that is in dispute. Or it is a question of the theology espoused by a specific rabbi and that rabbi's approach to halachic interpretation.

There is, then, an inherently arbitrary quality to the exercise of rabbinic authority. Yet that is the price we have to pay for keeping the system vital and creative. The Torah itself refuses, indeed God refuses, to lock us into a hermetically closed system; that would be its doom. But then God has to accept the limitations on God's own power that this position implies. That is the message of the postscript to the frequently invoked Talmudic story of Akhnai's oven. The story (as related in *Bava Metziah* 59b) involves a dispute between Rabbi Eliezer and the majority of rabbinic sages. Rabbi Eliezer refuses to accept the majority ruling and invokes a series of miracles designed to convince his colleagues that his position is correct. When these fail, Rabbi Eliezer calls for the support of a heavenly voice; it proclaims that the halachah is according to Rabbi Eliezer. Whereupon the head of the court, Rabbi Joshua, stands and quotes Deuteronomy 30:12: "It [the Torah] is not in the heavens!" In the postscript to the story, one of the sages later encounters Elijah and asks for God's reaction to the incident. "God laughed and said, 'My children have defeated me; my children have defeated me.'"

It is clear from the story that the "correct"—that is, in an absolute sense—ruling was Rabbi Eliezer's. It is also clear that this correct ruling is totally irrelevant. Since the Torah is no longer in the heavens, the law is whatever the human court determines it to be. And God has to live with that.

Our situation today is confusing, for we no longer have a single rabbinic court, nor do we hear heavenly voices. Our rabbinic authorities, then, must recognize that their situation is tension ridden. They have broad authority to rule according to their own most informed reading of the Torah, but they also must recognize that although their authority is grounded in God's will, none of them knows explicitly what God may or may not want on any specific issue. Nor is what God wants even relevant to the issue, for the Torah is "not in the heavens."

To lose sight of that tension, either by disclaiming the authority rabbis legitimately have or by claiming that their rulings have explicit divine backing, is perilous. It is our guarantee that Judaism will enjoy continued vitality and creativity.

In the Presence of a King

THE TWENTY-FIFTH CHAPTER OF LEVITICUS is the single most powerful statement of social policy in the Torah. The chapter begins with laws regarding the seventh, or sabbatical, and the fiftieth, or jubilee, years. The underlying theme of these laws is expressed in verse 23: "For the land is Mine; you are but sojourners and residents with Me."

Because the land of Canaan belongs to God, and because it is given to the Israelites as a temporary possession, God's concern extends over human ownership of portions of the land and over how the land is to be used. It cannot be disposed of in perpetuity, and every seventh year the land, too, must be allowed to enjoy its Sabbath. Effectively, then, conditions regarding land ownership are brought within the framework of the broader social concerns of Torah.

There then follows a series of laws, each beginning with the phrase "If your kinsman becomes impoverished" and continuing with the circumstance: is forced to sell his land, becomes indebted to you, becomes indentured to you, becomes indentured to a non-Israelite. In each of these cases we are instructed as to how to treat that impoverished kinsman to maintain his dignity and, even more, to help him emerge from his impoverished state.

Scattered through the chapter are a series of striking comments: We are all servants to God and must not become servants to other human beings. We must not rule ruthlessly over any other Israelite. We must not extract interest for loans. Our kinsman must live with us, by our side.

Running through the chapter are two refrains: "I am the Lord your God" and "Revere your God." The ultimate theological grounding for all of this social legislation is simply that there is a God in the world, that we live continuously in the presence of God, and that God's reign over us demands a certain kind of social structure on earth. There is a majestic quality to these refrains. They occur here in a specific context, reminding us of the impulse behind our social policies, but they also serve as the underlying consciousness that should inform our entire life experience as Jews.

The most striking elaboration of that sense of living our entire lives in the presence of God occurs in the very opening paragraph of the *Shulchan Aruch,* the sixteenth-century code of Jewish law that serves to this day as the most recent and most authoritative codification of the corpus of Jewish law, at least for the Ashkenazi community. The *Shulchan Aruch* was composed by Rabbi Joseph Karo in Palestine, but it became authoritative for European Jews because of the work of an eminent Polish rabbi, Moses Isserles, who incorporated the practices and customs of German and Polish Jews when they clashed with the Spanish rites followed by Rabbi Karo.

The passage I recall is Rabbi Isserles' addendum to the first paragraph of Rabbi Karo's code, a paragraph dealing appropriately enough with how we must conduct ourselves when we arise in the morning.

> The manner in which a person sits, moves about, and pursues his affairs when he is alone at home is not the same as the manner in which he would sit, move about, and pursue his affairs when he is in the presence of a great king. Neither is his speech and his uninhibited way of talking in the presence of his family or his relatives as his speech would be in the presence of the king.
>
> Consequently, if one realizes that the Great King, the Holy One Blessed be He, Whose glory fills the entire universe, is standing before him and sees all he does ... the submission and reverence that stems from his awe of God will touch him and he will feel constantly disconcerted before God, but he will never feel disconcerted in the presence of other people who mock him for his service to God.

Some thoughts about this passage. First, it is thoroughly uncharacteristic of Rabbi Isserles's other comments in that it is not itself a statement of law. Its placement at the very beginning of the code identifies itself for what it is: an attempt to capture the sensibility that inspires not only the work as a whole, but even more the kind of life experience the code is designed to create.

Second, it would be a mistake to become excessively preoccupied with the implicit theology of the statement. In fact, Rabbi Isserles's statement is not a theological claim at all. It assumes a certain theological position, but it is much more an attempt to impress us with the impact our theology should have on our life experiences as Jews.

However we conceive of God, then, to live within the framework of Jewish religion is to fashion our lives from the awareness that we live in the presence of God. That awareness makes a difference in how we treat other people and how, to quote Rabbi Isserles, we talk and conduct all of our affairs. If anything, his statement is designed to remind us that obeying the infinite details of Jewish law as elaborated in the *Shulchan Aruch* is simply not an end in itself. That is surely its most important purpose, for we all too easily lose such awareness when we become preoccupied with doing the right thing.

Sure, we should do the right thing, but not simply because it is recorded in the book. Rather, we do it as a way of coming close to, and remaining aware of, the presence of God in the world and in our lives. To remember that is the challenge.

The Fanatic

W HAT'S SO GREAT ABOUT PINCHAS? The single most significant issue arising from the Torah portion named for him
is the morality of his killing of a Jew and a non-Jew who were
cohabiting in defiance of God's law.

The terms that are commonly used to describe Pinchas are
"passionate" and "zealous." My dictionary defines the latter as a
"fanatically committed person." Pinchas, in his impassioned and
zealous defense of God's honor, took the law into his own hands,
slaughtering the offending Israelite prince, Zimri, and his Midianite woman, Cozbi, thus stemming God's punishment of the
Israelites for cohabiting with foreign women.

God clearly approves of Pinchas' act. That's why God
rewards him with a "pact of friendship" and "a pact of priest-
hood for all time." But even in the Bible itself, we begin to see
some distancing from the more gory aspects of Pinchas's act of
vengeance. Psalm 106:30 captures the episode in one verse: "Pinchas stepped forth and intervened, and the plague ceased." Jacob
Milgrom notes that "intervened" here—the Hebrew is *vayepal-*

lel—can only mean "mediation by prayer." There is not a word here about the killing, or about passion and zeal.

Not unexpectedly, the Rabbis were even more uncomfortable with the act because, above all, they were very much concerned with preserving legitimate and authoritative legal and communal structures. They could not possibly tolerate a group of Pinchas-types who would act on their own intuitive authority.

The rabbinic discussion of Pinchas' action progressively narrows the range of its application. Had Pinchas consulted a *beit din*, a rabbinical court, they would have refused him permission. Had he killed his victims before or after the act, he would have been executed for murder. Had his victim anticipated Pinchas and turned on him in self-defense, he would not have been guilty of homicide.

This later spin on our narrative rests on the assumption that according to Talmudic law, the offending Israelite prince should not have been punished in this way. The midrash adds that the authorities might have sought to excommunicate Pinchas, were it not for God's intervention by establishing an eternal covenant with him.

A further question intrudes. Why is it that Moses himself did not take action in this instance, and what was Moses' own reaction to this deed? Could it possibly be because Moses himself, much earlier in his career, slaughtered a man on his own authority (Ex. 2:12)? My sense is that Moses understood well the nature of Pinchas' passionate zeal, and was, on some level of consciousness, uncomfortable with it.

The Rabbis may well have shared Moses' discomfort, but they also acted to keep the heroic dimension of Pinchas's act in our awareness, typically by including him in a significant liturgical moment. Whenever a Jewish child is circumcised, three characters are introduced into the room via the liturgy: Abraham, Pinchas, and Elijah. Superficially, we can explain this grouping by noting that in each of the narratives where these personalities appear, the word *brit*, "covenant," is used, and what is transpiring before us is of course the *brit* ritual par excellence.

However, on a deeper level, what unites these three personalities is that each was a passionate zealot, each was a fanatic. Think of Abraham, who is identified above all as *ne'eman*, or "loyal"—loyal enough to be willing to sacrifice his son at God's command. Consider Elijah, who reminds God that he is moved "by zeal for the Lord ... for the Israelites have forsaken Your covenant, torn down Your altars, and put Your prophets to the sword. I alone am left, and they are out to take my life" (I Kings 19:10). And then think of Pinchas.

That striking verse, "I alone am left," explains it all. The fanatic is convinced that the established social and legal structures have collapsed, that anarchy rules, and that he alone is left to right the wrongs that abound about him. In effect, anarchy is to be responded to with anarchy.

It's not surprising that these three fanatics are invoked at every *brit*. There is an element of fanaticism about the way our people has held on to that ritual throughout our history and in every possible life situation, and the tradition wants to remind us of that. Further, it is fascinating to note that the later tradition identifies Pinchas with Elijah, for both were zealous for the honor of God. Elijah, in fact, is assigned the honor of proclaiming the coming of the Messiah. No small honor, that.

The final word, then, is ambivalence. The *Torah Temimah*, commenting on the rabbinic note that Pinchas would have been excommunicated had God not intervened, suggests that it all hangs on motivation, and human motivations are never quite clear—particularly to the one who acts. Since our motivation is never clear, he adds, we simply cannot permit people to take the law into their own hands and go around killing people of whose behavior they disapprove. So even though we invite Pinchas to every *brit*, and even though God has given him a pact of eternal friendship, the Rabbis seem to say, don't emulate his behavior. Society cannot tolerate Pinchas, for it cannot tolerate anarchy.

I am left also with those poignant words uttered by Elijah. "I alone am left, and they are out to take my life." It is the ultimate loneliness of the zealot and his paranoia that terrify us. If we understand that, we will begin to understand the roots of political and religious fanaticism and begin to learn how to deal with it.

Cosmos and Chaos

W HETHER OR NOT GOD CREATED THE WORLD out of noth- ing—a major issue among medieval philosophers—is clearly not an issue in the Bible itself.

As Rashi points out, the first verse of the Bible must be trans- lated not as "In the beginning, God created heaven and earth," but rather "When God began to create heaven and earth"; that opening is followed by a long parenthetical clause, "the earth being unformed and void, with darkness over the surface of the deep and a wind from God sweeping over the water."

The plain sense of the text, then, is that at the outset there was darkness, deep waters, and wind; all was in a state of *tohu vavohu*, which Rashi explains by using an early French word for "dizziness," what we feel when things seem to be swirling about us. God then creates light, separates light from darkness, and calls the light "day" and the darkness "night."

Note that the narrative does not tell us that God created darkness. What God does create is light, separating out light from the prevailing darkness. God also does not create the waters but rather creates the expanse of the sky that separates the water above the sky from the water below the sky, and then gathers (that is, separates) the water below the sky into the seas so dry land may appear.

Thus the biblical model of creation is not something out of nothing but rather order out of anarchy or cosmos out of chaos. God's creative work is one of structuring. Note the frequent appearance of the verb "separate" in these passages.

In this creation story, the literary structure mirrors the structuring of the created world. Each piece of creation is accorded a day, and the story of each day is captured in a passage that begins and ends the same way: "God said" at the outset, and "there was evening and there was morning, a second [or third, etc.] day" at the end. This literary structure reinforces the message of the text, which is that God introduces structures throughout creation: Everything is assigned its place.

God does not abolish darkness and the deep waters but rather their potentially anarchic quality. Later, in the account of the flood, we are told that "the fountains of the great deep burst apart, and the floodgates of heaven broke open."

At the flood, God allows the controls that were established over the waters to collapse; all the structures of creation disappear, and the water covers all of creation once again. The flood thus marks a return to the early state of chaos—punishment for the social chaos introduced into the world by human beings.

The story of these early chapters of the Torah is one of tension between cosmos and chaos—a recurrent theme throughout the Torah. God's promise to Noah never again to flood the earth is accompanied by the first code of law, the Noahide commands; it is followed by God's covenant with Abraham and the covenant at Sinai.

In each case, the covenant is predicated on the acceptance of law, the classic Jewish way of structuring human life. The underlying assumption is that both God and humanity are involved in the struggle to maintain a sense of cosmos in the world. But that is not a simple task. The original ordered world created by God lasted but a biblical week. Paradigmatic human beings then enter into the picture—Adam and Eve, Cain and Abel. This marks the beginning of history as the Bible understands it, for they, of course, are us.

The age of history is characterized by an unremitting tension between cosmos and chaos. In the Bible, there is a cause-and-effect relationship between the chaos humans introduce into the world and the chaos marking God's response, but that belief is much more problematic for us than for the Bible.

That tension between cosmos and chaos remains indelibly part of our day-to-day existence. Sure, there is a basic sense of cosmos out there—the sun rises and sets, seasons follow seasons, there is *shalom* (which, in this context, means "order" or "integrity") in the heavens, and nature as a whole manifests a startling pattern of order. And most of us human beings work mightily to ensure that our social structures will be maintained as well.

But inevitably, chaos erupts: floods, earthquakes, and hurricanes; sudden coronaries and leukemia; homicides and holocausts. We have not succeeded in creating a totally ordered social structure, nor has God banished the forces of chaos. We recall then that God did not abolish the darkness but put it in its proper place.

Our consolation is Shabbat. That first Shabbat, a day that is also "separated" from the other days of the week, is itself the embodiment of total cosmos. The later tradition tell us that Shabbat is both a remembrance of creation and a foretaste of the age-to-come, when the age of history will reach an end. It is our fleeting experience of what it must have been like in the cosmos that was, and of what it will be like in the cosmos-to-come, when all of chaos will be banished, both from history and from nature, forevermore.

Moments of Darkness

THE NINTH PLAGUE, THE PLAGUE OF DARKNESS, fascinates. This darkness was not simply the absence of light. It had a positive quality to it; it could be felt. It had substance, and it lasted for three days. This darkness "descended upon all the land of Egypt," yet "all the Israelites enjoyed light in their dwellings" (Ex. 10:22–23).

Nahum Sarna, in his Jewish Publication Society commentary to Exodus, ascribes the darkness to the scorching sirocco wind that envelops the land in thick sand and dust, blackening out the sky. We can appreciate Sarna's attempt to explain the plague, to give it a thoroughly natural cause. That may be comforting to some of us. However, it dismisses the miraculous nature of the plague, that it was precisely God's intervention into nature. Besides, scorching winds would not discriminate between Egyptian homes and their neighboring Israelite homes that enjoyed light.

Nevertheless, when it comes to light and darkness, discrimination is the heart of the issue. God's creation of the world began with God's separating the light from the preexisting darkness (Gen. 1:4). And a passage from Isaiah (45:7), which we echo in a somewhat revised form in our Shacharit service, has God claiming (in contradiction to Genesis), "I form light and create darkness, I make *shalom* and create woe." Here, light and darkness become metaphors for cosmos and chaos. God creates both and separates one from the other.

Finally, in what is undeniably a reflection of this ninth plague, after Mordechai and Esther succeed in saving their compatriots from Haman's evil decree, we are told that "the Jews enjoyed light and gladness, happiness and honor" (Esther 8:16). Here, as well, light is a metaphor for security and well-being, for order and harmony.

Darkness in and of itself can be either comforting or terrifying. For some of us at certain times, darkness relieves us of the tensions associated with our lives in the world of light. But darkness can also be a source of tension, a state when our fears get the better of us, a time for nightmares.

Perhaps, then, the light-darkness distinction in the ninth plague should also be understood as metaphor. For the Egyptians, the darkness reflects their terror of the disaster to come; for the Israelites, the light reflects the joy of their approaching redemption.

This is a familiar pattern in the Bible: certain words are used in widely different contexts to illuminate each other. The same pattern emerges from an apparently innocent detail in the description of the ninth plague: it lasted three days, we are told twice, in two successive verses.

Where else are we told about a three-day interval? In a number of places, most strikingly in the *Akedah* story of the binding of Isaac and later in preparation for the revelation at Sinai. Abraham and Isaac saw the place that God had designated for the sacrifice from afar, precisely on the third day of their journey. And at Sinai, the revelation took place on the third day after the Israelites arrived there.

In the *Akedah* narrative, the three days extend the tension of the story. Why did it take three days? Why this detail in a story that has almost no details? What happened during these three days? What did Abraham feel during this journey? What did Isaac feel? The text tells us not a word.

The three days of the plague of darkness could also be a metaphor for the Egyptian experience of darkness, the nightmarish terror that we feel as the story of the plagues reaches its climax.

And the three days at Sinai? We are told that God came down on Sinai in a dense cloud that clothed the mountaintop. Sinai was all in smoke, "for the smoke rose like the smoke of a kiln" (Ex. 19:9–18).

Cloud and smoke are revealing metaphors for the event itself. The entire description of the revelation is ambiguous. If you read it carefully, it is never totally clear what happens and in what order; it takes place as if in a cloud. And it inspires terror; the people say, "Let not God speak to us, lest we die" (Ex. 20:16). Moses alone enters the cloud.

The three days at Sinai evoke the three days of Egyptian darkness, except now the Israelites are in a darkness reflecting the mystery, the awesome nature of the event, the tension that envelops the community. For they, too, know that after this event they will never be the same. But what will they become? What lies ahead for them? How could they contemplate this event without a sense of tension, even terror? Their past was at least familiar; the future was uncertain. It, too, lay in darkness.

Not only the Egyptians, then, but also Israel experienced periods of darkness. Light and darkness serve as a set of polarities that characterize all human experience. We as individuals and as communities constantly live with alternating moments of light and darkness, not only in the physical sense, but also as metaphors for security and vulnerability, cosmos and chaos.

A Written Record

DID MOSES WRITE THE TORAH? The conventional, traditional belief is that he did write it all, with the possible exception of the last eight verses that describe his death. Those were penned by his successor, Joshua.

Nevertheless, in the entire Torah there are only three specific references to Moses' writing anything. The first is in Exodus 24:4, in *Parashat Mishpatim*. Moses repeats God's commands to the people, they commit themselves to obey, and "Moses then wrote down all the commands of the Lord."

But what precisely did Moses write here? The text says that he wrote God's commands. This implies that he wrote down what the seventh verse calls "the book of the Covenant." That is, he recorded the account of God's covenant with Israel and the code of law spelling out in concrete detail what it means for Israel to be covenanted to God, beginning with the Ten Commandments in Exodus 20 and continuing through the end of Exodus 23.

The second two references are at the very end of Deuteronomy, shortly before Moses' death. Deuteronomy 31:9 has Moses writing down what the Hebrew calls *HaTorah* (literally "this Teaching"), and a few verses later, this book of Teaching is deposited beside the Ark of the Covenant. Further, in this same chapter, we are told that Moses wrote down the words of a poem. The poem is surely the one sung in the very next chapter. But what about "this Teaching," or *HaTorah*?

Here, traditionalist scholars and modern Bible critics part company. The latter say that what Moses wrote was probably the book of Deuteronomy (or portions of it). The traditionalists use this verse to claim that Moses wrote the entire Torah from Genesis "to the very end," except for the story of his death in Deuteronomy 34:5–12. Thus we have the foundational doctrine that God dictated the entire Torah, that Moses wrote it all down in one single, coherent document, and that this is the text we have before us to this day. For one explicit statement of this position, see Nachmanides' introduction to his Torah commentary.

This controversy raises serious theological issues to be explored elsewhere. But what interests me is the insistence that there must be some kind of written record of God's will, as well as the additional note that it must be read aloud to the assembled community.

Exodus 24:7 has Moses reading "the record of the covenant" aloud to the people. Deuteronomy 31:10–11 instructs the priests and the elders to read the book of Teaching to all of Israel in every seventh year during the Sukkot festival. The Mishnah (*Sotah* 7:8) reflects this practice. And Deuteronomy 31:30 has Moses reciting the poem again "to the very end, in the hearing of the whole congregation of Israel."

However we understand what it was that Moses wrote, it is clear that whatever was written was read aloud to the entire congregation. This is the ultimate source of our practice, traditionally traced back to Ezra, of reading the Torah aloud on four separate occasions each week, as well as on Rosh Chodesh, festivals, and fast days.

The Bible preserves other records of reading some Torah text aloud to the community. Second Kings 23:2 says King Josiah read "the entire text of the covenant scroll" that had just been discovered (probably a reference to Deuteronomy), to the assembled community. In Nehemiah 8:1–3, Ezra brings "the scroll of the Teaching of Moses with which the Lord had charged Israel," and he "read from it ... from the first light until midday ... to the men and the women and those who could understand." In each of these cases, the reading leads to a renewal of the covenant between God and Israel.

So much of our understanding of Judaism rests on these principles. We commonly say that Judaism is a text-based religion, that the will of God for Israel is canonized in a text, that the primary mitzvah is the study of Torah, that we have the responsibility to teach it constantly to our children, and that the ideal Jew is a studying Jew. All of these distinctive characteristics of Jewish religion stem from the belief that God's will was written down and then read aloud to the assembled community.

That is why, for this Jew at least, the Torah reading in the synagogue is the very heart of worship. This is public education with vigor. Weekly, in fact almost daily, we hear the words of the Torah. Every Torah reading is for me a reenactment of Sinai. Deuteronomy 29:13–14 insists that God's covenant was established not only with those present that day but also with "those who are not with us here this day." So I, too, was at Sinai. Whenever I attend to the Torah reading, I fully understand that claim.

PART IV

Suffering, Death, and Redemption

The Challenge of Job

THE MAJOR PART OF CHAPTER 26 of Leviticus is an extended list of blessings and threats—blessings that will follow Israel's obedience to God's commands, and threats that will follow Israel's flouting of those commands. The blessings take up eleven verses, the threats thirty verses.

In the synagogue, these thirty verses are customarily read rapidly and in a hushed voice, as if to minimize their horror. A longer and even more vivid list of blessings and threats is found in Deuteronomy 28. It, too, is read rapidly and in a hushed voice.

The theological principle that underlies these passages is explicit. It is the traditional Torah explanation for the most baffling challenge to believers in every religious community, the challenge that haunts every human life: the pervasiveness of suffering. For the believer, the question is: How can a just, omnipotent, and compassionate God cause or tolerate human suffering?

The answer: Suffering is God's punishment for sin. From within this biblical mind-set, nothing that happens in the world happens randomly. If God's will is sovereign, and if God is just, then suffering must be purposeful and justified. This response vindicates God's judgment.

That formula is explicit in our passage. It begins in Leviticus 26:3: "If you follow My laws and faithfully observe My commandments, I will grant your rains in their season." It continues in verses 14–16: "But if you do not obey Me and do not observe all these commandments ... I will wreak misery upon you." The details of the "misery" follow.

The main problem with this answer is that it is defied by our experience. The Bible itself recognizes that. One entire biblical book, Job, explicitly rejects it. Job was a perfectly righteous man. Satan challenges God: Job was righteous, Satan claims, only because God has blessed him with health and prosperity. Take away his possessions and injure him, and he will quickly reject God. God frees Satan to make Job suffer, which he does, but Job never rejects God.

Job's friends arrive and offer the traditional argument: Job must have sinned to merit such suffering. But Job rejects that argument and maintains his innocence. He has not sinned, certainly not sinned sufficiently to merit such suffering. At the very end of the book (chapter 42), God restores Job's fortunes and tells Job that he was right all along, that his suffering had nothing to do with any sinful behavior on his part. In fact, God is "incensed" at Job's friends for not having "spoken the truth about Me as did My servant Job." If Job will pray on their behalf, God will forgive them.

Something astounding has occurred here: The Bible subverts itself. In fact, God rejects God's own teaching. In an act of colossal theological chutzpah, an anonymous author stands a central traditional biblical doctrine on its head and has God explicitly reject it. True, God never does tell Job precisely why he suffered. Also true, we now have to deal with a God who makes a righteous man suffer simply to win a bet with Satan.

How are we to worship this God? And even more, we must wonder, what is this book doing in the Bible in the first place? These questions, and many more, make this book among the most fascinating and difficult in the Bible. But to return to our point, the author of Job clearly was aware that the traditional doctrine didn't always work. His personal experience confounded it, and he allows his personal experience to win out over the tradition. He clearly was aware that it is not only sinful people who suffer. In fact, sometimes the very opposite is the case: Sinful people seem to prosper. And he also knew that far too frequently, perfectly righteous people suffer terribly. Our personal experience confirms all of this.

What is equally astounding is the fact that despite the clear message of Job, the traditional doctrine continues to be invoked to this day. To the horror of many, some right-wing Jewish circles insist the Holocaust must be understood as God's punishment for the "sins" of European Jewry—"sins" such as Zionism, the Enlightenment, assimilation, Reform and Conservative Judaism, and others.

I learn three lessons from this inquiry. First, the Bible is not one book but an anthology, or, even more, a library consisting of many books. One does not expect all the books in a library to agree with one another. Second, it is perfectly legitimate for us to bring our personal experience to bear against a traditional doctrine, even if it leads us to abandon that doctrine. The author of Job does precisely that, and the book was canonized. Finally, the pervasiveness of human suffering, particularly the suffering of righteous men and women, is the ultimate mystery, the ultimate challenge to faith. There is no easy resolution to that dilemma.

Suffering and Redemption

O NE IMPLICIT AND TWO EXPLICIT theological issues pervade the Torah portion of *Vayera*. Ultimately, they are all one.

First, a note on the parashah break. The Torah portion for *Shemot*, the portion prior to *Vayera*, does not end with the last verse of Exodus chapter 5, which convention might have dictated, but rather with the first verse of chapter 6. The division of the biblical text into chapters was done by Christians, but the parashah breaks were the work of the Rabbis, and they never end a parashah, or for that matter even an aliyah, on a down note. The last verse of chapter 5 is the despairing accusation by Moses that God has not redeemed Israel from bondage. God forbid that we should live for an entire week with that complaint ringing in our ears! Exodus 6:1, in contrast, conveys God's promise to redeem. That we can live with for a week.

The two explicit issues are, first, the mysterious reference to God's two names in the opening verses of the parashah, and the second, God's depriving Pharaoh of his freedom by "hardening his heart."

·I have never been troubled excessively by God's hardening Pharaoh's heart. The conventional interpretation is that God did not deprive Pharaoh of his freedom until he had hardened his heart on his own. God uses our natural inclinations for God's own purposes. But this case is precisely the exception that proves the rule. There is no more powerful demonstration of the fact that God created all of us with the freedom to choose to do good or ill than in this one singular case, in which God had to intervene decisively to deprive one human being of that freedom. More important, that's precisely why the Torah informs us again and again that in this specific case, this was God's doing. Why, in this case, did God deprive Pharaoh of his freedom? For one reason only: to demonstrate God's power to redeem.

Nor am I excessively troubled by the mysterious reference to God's multiple names at the very beginning of the parashah: "And Elohim [God] said to Moses ... I am Adonai; I appeared to Abraham, Isaac, and Jacob as *El Shaddai,* but by My name YHVH I did not make Myself known to them" (Ex. 6:2–3).

God has many names throughout the Torah, and in fact, God's supposedly "new" four-letter name [YHVH] has appeared many times prior to this. Also, if this name was previously unknown to the Israelites, its appearance now would scarcely promote the credibility of God's promises to redeem, which is precisely the point of God's promise to Moses.

Here, then, the conventional interpretation is probably as close as we can get to deciphering this enigmatic statement. What is "new" now is a previously unknown manifestation of God's power to redeem on a massive scale. Until now, God's functioning in history has been restricted to an extended family. But early in the book of Exodus (1:8), a new entity enters on the scene: *am B'nei Yisrael.* The Israelite people, not simply an extended family, becomes the locus of God's activity. God will now redeem an entire people. This new manifestation of God's redemptive power demands a new face of God, and with this new face comes a new name. As always, in Torah, the name is the person.

Finally, the implicit issue that pervades the entire parashah: Why the Egyptian bondage? Why the suffering? Why the oppression in the first place? Why was this necessary? The closest the Torah comes to providing an answer is its numerous references to the fact that because Israel has known oppression, it must never itself become an oppressor.

But there is an additional answer to the question. The experience of bondage was required to demonstrate God's power to redeem. God does many things: God creates, God reveals, and God redeems. That theological trilogy is echoed throughout Judaism's later theological tradition, for example, in the blessings surrounding the recitation of the Shema in the morning and evening liturgies. Each of these manifestations of God's power finds its paradigmatic expression in the Bible.

What is most noteworthy about God's redemption of our ancestors from Egypt is that in the later tradition, it becomes the guarantee for God's eventual redemption from all of the oppressions imposed upon us throughout history. As God redeemed us then, so will God redeem us once again at the end of days. That is why this parashah begins not with Moses' cry of despair, but with God's promise of redemption. All of our issues are ultimately one.

Private and Public

THE TENSION BETWEEN THE INDIVIDUAL and the collective, between the private and the public, is a central theme toward the end of the Torah.

The Torah portion *Nitzavim* begins with a widely inclusive statement: "You stand this day, all of you before the Lord your God" (Deut. 29:9), and then specifies who the "all of you" includes: tribal heads, elders, all the men of Israel, children, wives, even strangers within the gates. (Our modern sensibility is offended because "wives" are specified as opposed to "women," the precise parallel to "all the men of Israel." Women are identified only by their relationship to a spouse. But where does the single woman fit in?) Two verses later, the range is extended even further: God makes this covenant "not with you alone, but both with those who are with us here this day and with those who are not with us here this day" (Deut. 29:13–14).

I am perpetually astounded by this claim. Moses is clearly not referring to those who were living but not present at that very moment. He can only be referring to all the descendants of that community to the end of time. The verse really means what it says: All of Israel throughout history is bound by God's covenant with our ancestors centuries ago, hence the sense of collective destiny that all Jews share. All of us were redeemed from Egypt (as our Passover Haggadah reminds us), stood at Sinai, wandered through the desert wilderness, entered the land of Israel, went into exile, and the rest. Israel's collective history is my history; Israel's collective destiny is my destiny.

This is the underlying assumption of the statement of biblical historiography that occupies much of the rest of the chapter. Israel's collective sin is to be punished collectively by the destruction of the land and the people, and by exile. But within this context, we find a singularly rare passage that refers to the individual: "Perchance there is among you some man or woman ... whose heart is even now turning away from the Lord our God.... When such a one hears the words of these sanctions, he may fancy himself immune.... the Lord will never forgive him" (Deut. 29:17–19).

The Chumash itself, in contrast to the rest of the *Tanakh*, rarely deals with the destiny of individuals, apart from notables such as Moses, who is punished for his individual transgression. At the heart of the pentateuchal narrative is the people Israel and their relationship to God. Here, however, God ignores the collective and singles out the individual for retribution. And though here "the Lord does not forgive," we know that the later tradition insists that the Lord certainly does forgive if the individual repents.

Then, at the very climax of the passage, comes one of the more mysterious verses in the entire Chumash: "Concealed acts concern the Lord our God; but with overt acts, it is for us and our children even to apply all the provisions of this teaching" (Deut. 29:28). What does this come from? What relevance does it have here?

Rashi's comment on this verse provides the answer. He has the Israelites protesting: "What can we do? You [God] punish the collective for the sins of the individual, but none of us knows the hidden thoughts of his fellow." To which God responds: "I do not punish you for the concealed acts; they concern God and God will exact punishment from the individual. But as for the overt acts, it is 'for us and our children' to banish the evil from [our] midst."

On no other occasion in the course of the year are we more aware of our belonging to the collective people of Israel than on the High Holy Days. We throng to our synagogues; we mingle with people we rarely see all year long. Our liturgy is in the plural. We say again and again, "*We* have sinned, *we* have transgressed, forgive *us,* pardon *us.*" Subliminally, we are aware throughout these hours that Jews around the world are doing precisely what we are doing, coming together in synagogues and chanting the familiar High Holy Days melodies.

Yet as I stand before my congregation on these days, I am starkly aware that this mass of people is composed of individuals, that each of us brings his or her own personal package into the synagogue and that each of these packages is unique. We bring with us our private pain, our personal triumphs, our individual guilt, and our singular resolves. We don't know what lies in the heart of the individual Jew sitting next to us; that is "concealed." What happens to these private agendas on the High Holy Days? How much of it gets articulated, clarified, resolved? How many of us leave the synagogue with much the same pain we entered with?

Our text is clear. We are collectively responsible for our communal failings, for Israel's failings are ours. We must confront them and banish them from our midst. Those are the "overt acts" for which God holds us responsible. That is a relatively simple task. As for our "concealed" failings, those that lie in our private hearts and souls, we are on our own. On these issues we must each of us deal with God, and that is much more complicated.

Still, we are not totally on our own. First, we are given this island in time, this ten-day period deliberately structured for introspection. Second, we are given a rich liturgy that offers ample clues as to what within ourselves we are to look for. We are also given the image of a God who reaches out to us, who wishes our turning even more than we do, who insists: "Turn to me and I will turn to you." For in Judaism, the moment of turning is a moment of mutual turning. The closing verse of Lamentations even assigns the initiative to God: "Take us back, O Lord, to Yourself, and let us come back; renew our days as of old."

Finally, we are given the awareness that however alone we feel, everyone around us is also alone. Everyone of us has an agenda. And in our shared aloneness, we can find a measure of support.

From Redemption to Reality

T HE FIGURE THAT FRAMES our celebration of Passover, the festival of our redemption, is Elijah.

Elijah appears at the beginning of the Passover season, at the climax of the haftarah from the book of Malachi; he reappears in our homes at the climax of our seder when we pour a cup of wine in his honor. But the feelings associated with Elijah's presence at each of these two moments are quite different.

On Shabbat HaGadol, Malachi prophecies that Elijah will appear "before the coming of the awesome, fearful day of the Lord." This passage is the source for the traditional belief that Elijah will announce the coming of the Messiah. Malachi is specific about what Elijah's presence will mean: "He shall reconcile parents with children and children with parents, so that, when I come, I do not strike the whole land with utter destruction" (Mal. 3:24).

Quite appropriately here, the messianic age is portrayed as a time of reconciliation, when all of the tensions that beset the current age of history will disappear. That Malachi emphasized the reconciliation of parents and children is a fascinating commentary on just how intractable these specific tensions can become. If Elijah can reconcile these tensions, he will reconcile all the other ones as well.

With this messianic vision in place, we then celebrate the festival of redemption wherein we reenact our passage, in the words of the Haggadah, "from slavery to freedom, from sorrow to joy, from mourning to festivity, from darkness to a great light, from subjection to redemption."

The reenactment of that journey from slavery to redemption is completed at the climax of the seder; as the Haggadah reminds us, our redemption from Egypt stands as the guarantor for our ultimate redemption to come. As God has redeemed us once before, so may God redeem us once again and enable us to celebrate other festivals, "joyous in the building of Your city and exultant in Your service." Elijah reappears in our homes just now because, for a moment, we can taste the presence of the Messiah in our midst, because we have been redeemed once again.

But now we do some curious things. We open our doors and we recite some terrifying passages from the Psalms and from the book of Lamentations. "Pour out Your wrath upon the nations that know You not ... For they have devoured Jacob and laid waste his habitations. Pour out Your indignation upon them and let the fierceness of Your anger overtake them. Pursue them in anger and destroy them from under the heavens of the Eternal."

Why do we open our doors? And why do we open them to say these terrifying things about God's anger toward the nations? If anything, we should close our doors when reciting these verses! And what does all of this have to do with the presence of Elijah at our tables and the whiff of the Messiah in our midst?

My sense is that the answers to all of these questions reflect our profound ambivalence about the coming of the Messiah. We

Jews are in an impossible position in regard to the messianic age. We pray for it constantly, we dream about it, we invoke its imminent coming; at the same time, we maintain a healthy suspicion about any possible sense that it has in fact arrived. We are warned against counting the days to the arrival of the Messiah and against forcing God's hand. Yet, however much the Messiah may tarry, we await the Messiah still.

Part of the reason for this ambivalence is that we have been burned far too often by false messiahs and the turmoil left in their wake. We also maintain a healthy awareness that however much we hope that the messianic age is at hand, a glance at the world reminds us that it still seems very far away. That is why at the climax of our seder, when Elijah is still in our homes and the dream of the ultimate redemption acquires an almost tangible presence, we open our doors and look out on the world. We are then reminded that the Messiah has not as yet really arrived. And we recall that just as our original redemption from Egypt required God's destruction of a past tyranny, so the ultimate redemption to come will involve God's active intercession against the tyrannies of today.

Elijah's presence in our homes at the seder catches our ambivalence in a very precise way. With one half of our brain, the part that enables us to dream, to have vision, to indulge in the imagination, we welcome the Messiah. But the part of the brain that demands that we confront reality as it is, that enables us to be detached, critical, and objective about our dreams, whispers that the age of history is still here. So we both invoke Elijah's presence and at the same time open our doors, glance out into the real world, and pray for the destruction of evil.

Opening our doors is our way of returning to history. It is much like the breaking of the glass at the climax of a wedding. The practice is less a recollection of tragedies past than an anticipation of tragedies to come. Here, we have just recited the last of the seven benedictions that describe Jeremiah's vision of the messianic age. Here again, for a brief moment, the Messiah is in our midst.

But just at that moment, we shatter the dream and return to the real world of history, where tensions and tragedies abound, and the messianic age seems far away. This tension between our dreams of a world perfected and a clear-eyed recognition of the imperfect world we live in today is one of the intractable tensions of our Jewishness. To be a Jew is to live with that tension.

Confronting Death
and Resurrection

O N YOM KIPPUR, WE ABSTAIN FROM FOOD AND DRINK, which sustain life, and from sex, which creates it. We wear the white *kittel*, the shroud in which we will be buried. We withdraw from the world of everyday life, and in sacred space, we create a world of sacred time, a world in which eternity rules and time stands still. We recite the Yizkor prayer and recall those close to us who have died.

Even more, we are acutely conscious of those who were among us last Yom Kippur and who are no longer here. We wonder which of us here today will not be here next Yom Kippur—and whether we, too, will be here next year. We consider that on this day it is sealed who will live and who will die. At the end of the day, we return to our homes to eat and drink. Four days later we celebrate Sukkot, the harvest festival.

Teshuvah, repentance, is a process of death and resurrection. Our familiar selves die, and we are reborn. We emerge from the day as newly born children, and a lifetime of new opportunities and challenges lies ahead of us.

The closing liturgical moments of the day are all eschatological. God alone is God. God's sovereignty is praised throughout all time, and we are in Jerusalem. The final sounding of the shofar announces the arrival of the Messiah and sends us back into history, for of course the Messiah has not, as yet, arrived. The world is not, as yet, fully redeemed, and the age of history, with all of its ambiguities, awaits us. However, we have been granted a whiff of immortality, one of those interim eschatological moments when, for the briefest of seconds, we can almost taste what it would be like to live in a world perfected.

Immediately following the shofar, we recite the everyday Ma'ariv prayer, beginning with the words, "The merciful God pardons sin and does not destroy." But we have just repented of all our sins! What sins remain, at this precise moment, for God to pardon? The obvious answer is: the sins that lie ahead. For as much as we are, at that moment, newborn children, the real world with all of its inevitable tensions lies before us.

Then we leave sacred space and sacred time, return to our homes, and begin to build our sukkah. This fragile booth, our temporary dwelling place, which is vulnerable to the elements and where the shadows overwhelm the sunlight, nevertheless serves as our source of security—the absolute paradigm of what it means to live as a Jew in an unredeemed world. Sukkot transports us out of eternity and back into time, for on Sukkot we celebrate both the cycles of nature and our ancestors' historical experience wandering in the desert.

Franz Rosenzweig, whose understanding of Yom Kippur is reflected in these thoughts, insists that on this day, we confront God in our loneliness. "Man is utterly alone on the day of his death" writes Rosenzweig. The prayers of these days "set him, lonely and naked, straight before the throne of God ... God will not ask about those around him and what they have done to help him, or corrupt him. He will be judged solely according to what he himself has done and thought."

Yom Kippur had particular meaning for Rosenzweig. It was on Yom Kippur—Oct. 11, 1913—when he was twenty-seven years old, that he entered a Berlin synagogue. He had made up his mind to follow the pattern of many of his friends and relatives and convert to Christianity, and he came to the synagogue to prepare himself for that conversion. Instead he emerged transformed. Rosenzweig wrote: "It no longer seems necessary to me, and therefore, being what I am, no longer possible [to convert]. I will remain a Jew!"

Nahum Glatzer, who was a member of Rosenzweig's intimate circle and who introduced his writings to the English-speaking world, notes that Rosenzweig never discussed precisely what transformed him on that Yom Kippur day. But the decisive moment may well have been a confrontation with his own mortality. More than anything else, it is our mortality that compels us to deal with the issue of the ultimate meaning of our lives, which in turn forces us to ask why we are here and what it is all about, and which ultimately may yield the faith that provides an orientation for life.

Rosenzweig writes as a classical existentialist, emphasizing our concrete and lonely individuality as the source of whatever meaning we are to wrest from life. Many modern Jewish theologians are troubled by Rosenzweig's sharp individualism. They claim that he fails to capture the essence of our liturgical experience; after all, we assemble on Yom Kippur, as on all Sabbaths and festivals, as a community. We pray in the plural for our communal sins and for communal forgiveness. Our dreams for a world redeemed include all of humanity.

Rosenzweig was not insensitive to the sense of community. His extended discussion of the cycle of the Jewish year centers on the experience of what he calls "the eternal people." But he insists that when we confront our own death—not death in the abstract, but my death, your death—we do so in ultimate loneliness. It is this very personal awareness of our own mortality that above all else forces us to grapple with the meaning of our existence, with the direction our lives have taken and may yet take in the days ahead.

On December 8, 1929, in his forty-fourth year, Rosenzweig died of amyotrophic lateral sclerosis. But on that Yom Kippur day in 1913, Rosenzweig experienced a personal death and resurrection.

Confronting Chaos

"IF ALONG THE ROAD, you chance upon a bird's nest, in any tree or on the ground, with fledglings or eggs and the mother sitting over the fledglings or on the eggs, do not take the mother together with her young. Let the mother go, and take only the young, in order that you may fare well and have a long life" (Deut. 22:6–7). Is there a biblical text more transparent, more direct in its impact, and more overflowing with pathos than this one? What else could the text possibly mean than that we are commanded to be sensitive to the feelings of animals—particularly when we read these verses in the context of other biblical passages: Do not plow with an ox and an ass in the same yoke (Deut. 22:10); do not slaughter an animal and its young on the same day (Lev. 22:28); do not muzzle an ox while threshing (Deut. 25:4).

Then there is that stunning last verse of the book of Jonah: God cares about Nineveh's animals! If we are to be that concerned about the feelings of an animal, how much more so about the feelings of a fellow human being? Maimonides explicitly interprets the text as reflecting God's concern for animals' feelings. Nachmanides and Ibn Ezra give it a different twist: It is directed to us, as the Torah's attempt to educate us in kindness.

But nothing in our tradition is ever simple. First, there is the Mishnah (*Brachot* 5:3 and *Megillah* 4:9), which teaches that one who is reciting the Amidah and adds "May Thy mercies extend to a bird's nest" is to be silenced. Why? According to one interpretation, it is because this person has wrongly assumed that God's command springs from compassion; rather, it is simply the decree of a sovereign God and must be obeyed as such. According to this reading, it is positively heretical to interpret our text as reflecting God's compassion. That's why the person has to be silenced, even in the midst of prayer.

The broader implication of this approach is that it is dangerous to try to enter the mind of God and figure out some kind of rational justification for God's commands. The danger is that should we later come across an instance when the reason doesn't seem to apply, we will then feel free to act differently. To take a flagrant example, if the biblical prohibition against eating pork were simply designed to prevent trichinosis, now that we have more refined cooking procedures, we should no longer be bound by that prohibition.

There is, then, only one good reason for letting the mother bird go, or for observing any mitzvah. God commanded us to do so, and we must obey God's command. Fortunately, this approach to the mitzvot never inhibited a healthy Jewish inclination to do the very opposite, to work at understanding and justifying God's commands, hence the sizable genre of *ta'amei hamitzvot* (reasons for the commandments) literature in our tradition. Still, the Mishnah's approach certainly does rob our text of its emotional impact.

Much more serious is the last clause of the passage. You are to let the mother go "in order that you may fare well and have a long life." Indeed! Do people who act sensitively to animals always fare well and enjoy a long life? Would that it were true! But it clearly is not, and then what do we do with the biblical promise of reward?

Our tradition preserves a devastating account of the impact on a sensitive, thinking Jew who saw this biblical promise contradicted. That man was Elisha ben Abuya, the Talmud's own scholar-apostate, who, following his apostasy, came to be nameless and known simply as *Acher*, "the Other One." What led Elisha to abandon his religious faith?

The Jerusalem Talmud (*Hagigah* 2:1) preserves various traditions on this question. In one of them, Elisha saw a man climb a tree and take the mother bird with her young, in violation of the Torah. The man descended the tree safely. The next day, he saw another man climb the tree, release the mother, and then take the young, as the Torah commands. When he descended, a snake bit him and he died.

Many of us encountered the story of Elisha ben Abuya in Milton Steinberg's *As a Driven Leaf*, a fictional treatment of Elisha's life. Here is Steinberg's account of the impact of the episode on Elisha:

> A great negation crystallized in him. The veil of deception dissolved before his eyes. The only belief he still cherished disintegrated as had all the others. The last tenuous chord that bound him to his people was severed....
>
> "It's all a lie," he said with a terrible quiet in his voice. "There is no reward. There is no Judge. There is no judgment. For there is no God."

This deceptively simple text raises nothing less than the most profound challenge facing religious faith. If to believe in God means to believe that the world manifests a fundamental order, an intrinsic justice, a sense of cosmos, then how do we deal with the blatant injustice, the incipient chaos that lurks on the fringes of our experience and periodically erupts into our world? How do we deal with an earthquake, a hurricane, an airplane crash, a child's death, and, of course, the Holocaust? What do we say to the Job-like persons in our communities?

Would that there were a simple answer to that question. But though we may never understand why bad things happen to good people, religion must at least provide us with the resources to respond to the chaotic in our life experience, to endure it, cope with it, and thereby restore a measure of order in the midst of the disorder. That is the acid test of every religion, a test that Judaism, with its range of such responses, seems to have passed.

For the wonder is not that there are Elishas in our midst, but that we all know so many who have retained their faith in the face of the most horrendous tragedies imaginable.

Ultimate Vulnerability

IN THE FINAL ANALYSIS, how much control do we really exercise over our destinies?

Most of us go through much of our lives without giving that question much thought. That's probably an indication of sound mental health. Were we obsessed with the awareness of our ultimate insecurity, we would probably lock ourselves in our rooms and sink into a deep depression.

But every now and then, we are shocked into the awareness that our vaunted control amounts to precious little. We become seriously ill, and we realize that our bodies' functioning is not entirely in our hands. We are laid off from work, and we realize how vulnerable our material resources really are. Our homes are flooded or destroyed by a tornado or an earthquake, and we become aware that we should never take for granted that we have a roof over our heads or food on our table.

It's at moments such as these, moments when the reality of our ultimate vulnerability hits home, that we become overwhelmed with gratitude for the blessings that we did or still continue to enjoy—for health and the health of those closest and dearest to us, for financial success, for the security of our homes, for the food.

The Torah reminds us of this ultimate vulnerability in a passage that is unrivaled in its simplicity and directness: "When you have eaten your fill, and have built fine houses to live in, and your herds and flocks have multiplied, and your silver and gold have increased, and everything you own has prospered, beware lest your heart grow haughty and you forget the Lord your God … and you say to yourselves, 'My own power and the might of my own hand have won this wealth for me'" (Deut. 8:12–17).

That's why we have to be reminded: "Remember that it is the Lord your God who gives you the power to get wealth" (Deut. 8:18). Our lives as Jews are studded with these reminders. When we arise in the morning and perform our bodily functions, we praise God, "who fashioned our body with wisdom and created openings and arteries, glands and organs, marvelous in structure, intricate in design. Should but one of them … fail to function, it would be impossible for us to exist even for a moment." We are reminded that even our bodies are not really ours to control.

The Bible instructs us that the first fruit of everything we produce belongs to God. Why? Ultimately because "the earth is the Lord's." We may think it's all ours, but ultimately it is God's. In biblical times, the first fruits of the herds were sacrificed or redeemed, and the first fruits of the fields were brought to the *kohanim,* or Temple priests, in Jerusalem.

Particular attention is paid to the firstborn male child, who also has to be redeemed. Why the firstborn male? Because we won our freedom from slavery in Egypt through the slaughter of the Egyptian firstborn males, and so we have to be reminded not to take even our children for granted. We acknowledge this through the ritual of *pidyon haben,* when we redeem our first-born sons. This rite of passage is frequently ignored because it has none of the power of the circumcision ritual that precedes it by three weeks. But within this broader context, this ritual conveys the striking message that nothing is ultimately our own, not even our children.

And that is why, in the passage immediately preceding the one quoted above, we are instructed: "When you have eaten your fill, give thanks to the Lord your God for the good land which God has given you." Therefore, we praise and thank God whenever we eat. We fulfill this mitzvah by reciting one of the forms of the Birkhat HaMazon, the blessing over food. For the Jew who lives a traditional liturgical life, there is no prayer more routine. We say it many times a day, often mindlessly, without attending to the words of the liturgy.

But the words are direct and powerful. We praise God, "who sustains the whole world with kindness and compassion." We thank God for our land, for our freedom, for our covenant, for the Torah, and "for the gift of life and compassion graciously granted us." And then we pray that "we may never find ourselves in need of gifts or loans from flesh and blood."

Ultimate vulnerability is an inevitable part of our human situation. The early chapters of Genesis describe how Adam and Eve, and later Cain—the paradigmatic human beings—were exiled as punishment for overstepping their assigned status. The point of these narratives is that according to Torah, exile is far more than a historical condition. It is also a metaphysical symbol for the human condition: To live a human life is to be in exile wherever one lives on the face of the earth. And to be in exile means to be ultimately homeless, insecure, and vulnerable, no matter how settled or "at home" we may seem to be. Cain's complaint that "anyone who meets me may kill me" (Gen. 4:14) is only slightly a hyperbole.

This state of ultimate vulnerability will end only with the coming of the Messiah. Until then, we must live with the peripheral awareness that our destinies are never totally under our control. And we must be grateful for those ritual and liturgical moments that remind us daily that we have much for which to be grateful.

Separations

THE FESTIVAL SHEMINI ATZERET is unique among biblical festivals in its lack of any distinctive theme or ritual. In the two biblical references to this day, Leviticus 23:36 and Numbers 29:35, the Jewish Publication Society translation offers the word *atzeret* as "sacred occasion," and in a footnote adds, "meaning of Hebrew uncertain."

Apart from that single word, we are commanded to celebrate this festival as we would any other: by refraining from work, by bringing appropriate sacrifices, and by holding a solemn gathering. Later, the prayer for rain was added to the liturgy of the day; it is the festival's single distinctive liturgical supplement.

In Israel, Shemini Atzeret and Simchat Torah are celebrated on the same day. But here in the diaspora, this festival is overshadowed by the pageantry of Sukkot, which ends the day before, and by the celebration of Simchat Torah on the day following.

Not unexpectedly, when the meaning of a biblical text is obscure, the rabbinic commentary is extraordinarily rich. The Rabbis read the word *atzeret* to mean "retain," "restrain," or "hold on to." Thus, Rashi (on the Leviticus passage) adds this touching homily: "This is like a king who has invited his children to a feast for so many days. When the time has come for them to leave, he says to them: 'My children, please stay another day. It's hard for me to part from you.'"

On this day, then, God, who has been celebrating with us for the seven days of Sukkot, pleads with us to stay another day because separating from us is difficult. Those whose children come home for the holidays and then prepare to return to their own homes understand God's feelings perfectly well.

Shemini Atzeret thus becomes the festival of both separation and resistance to separation. Suddenly, much of the distinctive mood of the day becomes clear. The holiday season is coming to an end; with some reluctance, we face the common year with no major festivals until Passover in the spring. Summer is at an end; fall and winter lie ahead. We are about to conclude the annual Torah reading cycle and to begin it again, a classic example of resistance to separation. We say Yizkor on this day and think of those dear to us from whom we have been separated by death, but whose presence is still palpable among us.

Yet life as a whole is one extended process of separating. Psychologists call it individuation. It begins with our separation from the mother's womb at birth and proceeds in stages from our childhood and adolescence through adulthood and old age, and to our ultimate separation: death.

Each of these stages is accompanied by fierce resistance, for though separation means greater independence, it also means ever greater vulnerability. There is a part of all of us that wants to be free and strong, and there is another part of us that wants to be nurtured and cared for. That tension is endemic to life itself. We can avoid neither the impulse to separate nor our resistance to it.

That same tension is also an inevitable dimension of our interpersonal relationships. We watch our infant children begin to walk, then go to school, leave home for college, and marry. We both rejoice in their growing independence and feel the wish to hold on a little longer. The pain we feel at their individuation is testimony to the power of the ties that bind us to them.

Death is very much in the air on this festival—the death that is part of the natural cycle, and the death of our loved ones that Yizkor brings to mind. It is appropriate, then, that the Torah reading for Simchat Torah includes the last verses of Deuteronomy that narrate the death of Moses.

The biblical account of Moses' death captures little of the drama that the event must have inspired. For that we must turn to the midrash and one of the most extraordinary pieces of rabbinic fantasy we have. It captures the struggle between Moses and God in which Moses argues that he should not have to die, or, at least, that he should not die now, prior to leading his people into the Promised Land, and God's refusal to allow Moses to live on.

Increasingly desperate, Moses pleads with heaven and earth, with the angels in the heavenly court, and with his disciple, Joshua, to intervene on his behalf. But God is adamant and orders the heavenly gates to be closed to prevent Moses' prayer from ascending on high. Moses even pleads to be allowed to live on as a beast or bird. God replies, "Moses, you are going to die because you are a descendent of Adam."

Finally, Moses makes peace with the divine decree, but when God orders his soul to leave his body, the soul rebels. Thereupon, in an astonishing peroration, God descends and draws Moses' soul out from his body with a kiss, the rabbinic reading of Deuteronomy 34:5, where Moses dies "at the command (al pi, or literally 'through the mouth') of God."

The struggle is placed in Moses' mouth, but it is the Rabbis who are speaking here. What they are expressing is the deeply human wish to cling to life and to resist death.

The final message of this festival is expressed in the words of Solomon, which are used for the haftarah for Shemini Atzeret. It is the conclusion of Solomon's address to his people upon completing the dedication of the Temple that he had built (I Kings 8:54–66).

Solomon concludes his address with this prayer: "May you be wholehearted with the Lord our God, to walk in God's ways and keep God's commandments, even as now." We are told that on this eighth day, the people bid good-bye to the king and returned to their homes, "joyful and glad of heart over all the goodness that the Lord had shown to God's servant David and God's people Israel."

Death Is Over

ONE OF THE GREAT DEATHBED SCENES in world literature concludes with these lines:

"It is all over," said someone standing beside him.
He heard these words, and repeated them in his soul.
"Death is over," he said to himself. "There is no more death."
He drew in a breath, broke off in the middle of it,
stretched himself out, and died.

When Tolstoy penned this description of the last seconds in the life of Ivan Ilyitch, he was drawing on a two-thousand-year-old tradition as to what happens to human beings after they die. From the second century BCE until the dawn of the modern age, Judaism and later Christianity affirmed that the death of a human being did not signify the end of that person's relationship with God, that God's power extended beyond the grave, that human beings would live again and come before God in judgment, and that at the end of days, death too would die.

Similarly, "death is over" is the message of that memorable last stanza of the "Chad Gadya" song we recite appropriately at the end of the Passover seder, which celebrates Israel's redemption from Egypt and also anticipates the future redemption to come. In that song, God is portrayed as slaughtering the Angel of Death. After that, indeed there will be no more death.

The two biblical personalities whose deathbed scenes are described in *Parashat Vayechi* did not have this tradition to draw on. The last words of Jacob and Joseph deal with what will happen to their bodies after they die. Jacob asks to be buried with his parents and grandparents in the cave of Machpelah, and Joseph asks that when God brings the Israelites into the Promised Land, his bones should accompany them.

If there is a hint of immortality in these scenes, it lies in Jacob's extended prophecy of what will happen to his sons in the days to come, and in Joseph's promise that God surely will bring God's people to their Promised Land. Jacob and Joseph's immortality is linked to the destiny of their progeny.

But neither Jacob nor Joseph, nor, for that matter, any other biblical personality, questions the finality of death. There are two exceptions to that claim: Elijah never really dies but is taken into heaven in a chariot (II Kings 2:11). Jewish folklore portrays him as reappearing on earth from time to time. Elijah also will herald the coming of the Messiah. The other exception is the early Genesis personality Enoch, of whom we are told that he walked with God and then was no more, for God took him (Gen. 5:24).

But none of the patriarchs—nor, for that matter, Aaron, Moses, or Miriam—is portrayed as expecting to live again after his death. In fact, the very opposite is the case. When Jacob is told of Joseph's apparent death, he refuses to be comforted: "No, I will go down mourning to my son in Sheol" (Gen. 37:35); and when his sons ask him to let them take Benjamin with them to Egypt, he replies: "My son must not go down with you, for his brother is dead and he alone is left. If he meets with disaster on the journey you are taking, you will send my white head down to Sheol in grief" (Gen. 42:38). Jacob has no hope of being reunited with his children after his death.

There are only two biblical texts that speak of the dead rising from their graves. One is Daniel 12:2 (usually dated from 165 BCE): "Many of those who sleep in the dust of the earth will awake." The other, of uncertain date, is Isaiah 26:19: "Oh, let Your dead revive! Let corpses arise!" This first phrase was later incorporated into our Amidah, where God is portrayed as *mechayei hametim,* "reviving the dead." That at the end God will destroy death seems also to be anticipated in Isaiah 25:8: "He will destroy death forever." God's future resurrection of the dead later became central to Pharisaic teaching, and once it was incorporated into the Amidah, the concept became canonical in Jewish thought until modernity.

A far more cynical deathbed scene is reflected in the haftarah for *Parashat Vayechi,* which describes the passing of King David (I Kings 2). David instructs his son Solomon to settle the score with his friends and enemies. Solomon is to reward those who were loyal to David and to kill his father's enemies. Echoing Jacob's fear, David urges Solomon not to let their white hair go down to Sheol in peace. There is none of the nobility of the Genesis death scenes in this passage. That it was still selected as the parashah's prophetic reading is a statement about the Rabbis' political realism.

My annual encounter with these deathbed scenes reminds me that it was on this Shabbat in 1972 that Rabbi Abraham Joshua Heschel died in his sleep. But literally days before he died, he taped the memorable television interview that was later shown on the Jewish Theological Seminary's *Eternal Light* program. That interview constitutes Rabbi Heschel's last words.

Many portions of that interview remain fresh in my mind, but two are worth recalling here. First, when Rabbi Heschel is asked what he anticipates will happen to him after he dies, he brushes aside the question. He has far too much to do during his lifetime; he is prepared to let God worry about what will happen to him after he dies.

The second is that remarkable last minute of the conversation, when Rabbi Heschel is asked if he has a message to deliver to young people. His answer: Remember that there is a meaning beyond the mystery, and that it is our responsibility to shape our lives as if they were a work of art.

I am always struck by the fact that death is so central to a Torah portion called *Vayechi,* "And he [Jacob] lived." The none-too-subtle message is that within death, life continues, in more ways than one.

Redeeming God

THERE IS NO QUESTIONING the joyous character of the Sukkot festival. Leviticus 23:40 instructs us that on this festival, we are to take the *lulav* and *etrog* and "rejoice before the Lord your God seven days." This is echoed in Deuteronomy 16:14–15, with the additional injunction to "have nothing but joy." In the Amidah and in the Kiddush, we identify this festival as *Z'man Simchatenu,* "Season of Our Joy."

But there is also a dark side to this festival of joy. We pray for rain. We dwell in a frail booth, unprotected from the elements of nature, where the shadow is to be greater than the light. We recite the book of Ecclesiastes, surely one of the bleakest books in the Bible. We will soon recite the Yizkor prayer for those who have departed this earth. And again and again, as we circle the Torah, waving our *lulav* and *etrog,* we plead for redemption, reciting, *Hosha Na!* "Save us! Help us! Redeem us! Rescue us!"

One of the prayers we use during these Hosha Na prayers is particularly puzzling. It reads, *Ani vaho hoshiah na.* What in the world do the first two words of this prayer mean?

The formula appears in the Mishnah (*Sukkah* 4:5) in the name of Rabbi Judah as an alternative to the more familiar *Anna Adonai hoshia na*, "Save us, God, we pray!" Most of the commentaries view the first two words of that strange prayer either as incorporating God's unpronounceable four-letter name or as being one of God's many names. It simply echoes the more familiar petition, "Save us, God, we pray."

But another comment suggests that we should understand the phrase as echoing a biblical verse, Psalm 91:15, which reads "I [God] will be with him in his distress." If this explanation is correct, then our obscure plea anticipates an equally puzzling passage in the long prayer that follows it in the Hosha Na liturgy: "As You saved [Israel] with the declaration, 'I [God] shall bring you forth [from Egypt],' which may be interpreted 'I [God] shall be brought forth with you [Israel],' save us!"

We know that God brought us out of Egypt. But in what sense was God brought out from Egypt with us? Was God enslaved in Egypt with us? If this interpretation is correct, our puzzling phrase acquires a strikingly new theological spin. It should be translated as "I and God, save us!" It seems to be saying, "Save us together!" "Save both of us!" We both [God and Israel] need to be saved, just as both of us were saved from Egypt.

The message of this prayer, then, is that both human beings and God need to be saved. And as we pray for our own salvation, we pray at the same time for God's salvation, for, as in the verse from Psalm 91, God is with us in our distress. God, too, needs to be saved.

But what can it mean to say that God is with us in our distress and that God needs to be saved? Can God really be in distress? Isn't God beyond distress? Does God really need to be redeemed?

Indeed. The overwhelming message of the Bible is that God is very much in distress, that God is vulnerable, that God needs people. The late Rabbi Heschel used to say that far from being all-powerful, the God of the Bible is totally frustrated. God never accomplishes what God wishes. The biblical saga is the story of God's wrestling with humanity, a story of God's failure to create the kind of world here on earth that God had hoped to create. It is the story of God's pain, pain mingled with infinite hope and yearning. The biblical God is indeed in search of people, to paraphrase the title of Heschel's most notable book.

A God who is dependent on people to be fully God is very much a God who is in distress and who needs to be redeemed, just as much as we do. So Sukkot recapitulates all of human history. It is a much more complicated festival than we might think. It is very much like life itself—rejoicing mingled with a hint of desperation, sunlight and shadow, thanksgiving and neediness, both human and divine.

From Cosmos to Chaos to Cosmos

T HE TRANSITION FROM THE FIRST BOOK of the Torah to the
second, from Genesis to Exodus, is marked very early in the
text. The narrative begins by listing the names of "the sons of
Israel," that is, the sons of Jacob/Israel. By the ninth sentence,
however, the new king of Egypt makes reference to "the Israelite
people." If Genesis is the story of a family, Exodus marks the
beginnings of the story of a people.

There is a second equally significant change in tone
between the two books. Genesis ends on a high. Jacob's sons
have been reconciled; Jacob and Joseph die peacefully; Joseph's
last words promise a return home to Canaan. The sense of closure is palpable. But just eight sentences into Exodus, the tone
grows ominous: A new king "who did not know Joseph" arises;
"the Israelite people" have become a threat; the oppression
begins.

Yet one of the great unsolved mysteries of the biblical narrative and, indeed, of Jewish religion as a whole remains: Why the

oppression? Why the slavery? Or, to paraphrase Rabbi Harold Kushner, why did such bad things happen to generations of our people who, as far as we know, were basically good people?

The branch of theology that deals with the problem of human suffering is called theodicy, literally "justifying (or vindicating) God's judgment." In much of the Bible—the book of Job is the most significant exception—suffering is understood as God's retribution for sin. Thus, the suffering is explained and God's justice is vindicated.

Although the Bible invokes this pattern time and again as a means of justifying much of the travail suffered by our ancestors in their early history, there is not a single explicit biblical suggestion that the Egyptian oppression should be understood as God's punishment. In fact, according to Genesis 50:20, the reason God ordained that the Israelites go to Egypt in the first place was for "the survival of many people" during a famine.

Further, the first reference to the Egyptian experience occurs in Genesis 15:13–16, in the context of God's covenant with Abraham. There, God accounts for the extended oppression in Egypt as a result of the fact that "the iniquity of the Amorites is not yet complete." In other words, God cannot redeem even God's own people until the time is ripe. That is hardly an acceptable justification for this suffering.

If there is no explicit theodicy for this experience, then we must look elsewhere for an explanation. The most compelling suggestion is echoed in an analysis of *The Wizard of Oz* published by Peter Steinfels, who writes on religion in the *New York Times*. Reporting on the address by Professor Paul Nathanson at an annual convention of the American Academy of Religion, Steinfels reflects on an ancient archetype, whereby an individual or a community is driven from its home, undergoes a prolonged period of wandering and struggle, then returns home wiser and more mature.

The Wizard of Oz provides a modern, popular version of this primitive archetype. Expelled from Kansas, Dorothy travels to Oz along the yellow brick road, where she has to struggle with the devious schemes of the Wicked Witch, and finally returns to Kansas again. In the meantime, she has learned the lessons of intelligence (from the Straw Man), compassion (from the Tin Man), and courage (from the Cowardly Lion).

On a much grander plane, this archetype appears in our tradition's tracing of the pattern whereby Adam and Eve are driven from Eden and forced to endure the trials and tensions of history, until, at the end of days, they return home to a totally harmonious existence in Eden. The pattern is from home to exile to home again, from harmony to tension to harmony, or from cosmos to chaos to cosmos. But that is precisely the pattern that structures Israelite history from Jacob through the conquest of Canaan under Joshua.

The ultimate explanation for the experience of Egyptian oppression, then, is not some past sin but rather some future expectation. Again and again, we are enjoined to remember how it felt to be a stranger and a slave in Egypt. That's why the Torah repeatedly tells us that we must treat the stranger and the slave with particular sensitivity, for "you know the feelings of the stranger, having yourselves been strangers in the land of Egypt" (Ex. 23:9).

Above all, the Exodus from Egypt is understood as God's paradigmatic act of redemption (Ex. 20:2 and Deut. 5:6). That's why we must remember the day of our departure from Egypt every day of our lives, which we do by reciting Numbers 15:37–41 as the concluding passage of the Shema, twice daily. Finally, every year, on the anniversary of the event, we reenact a piece of that journey, the passage from slavery to freedom, by telling the story of the Exodus at our Passover seder. The Mishnah (*Pesachim* 10:4) explicitly instructs that our telling of the story must embody the archetypal structure: We begin with disgrace (*g'nut*) and we end with glory *(sh'vach)*. What is the disgrace? We were slaves in Egypt. What is the glory? Our redemption from Egypt and the ultimate redemption still to come.

Note that the story is not simply that of our ancestors alone. It is our story as well. "We were slaves in Egypt" and, according to the Mishnah and the text of our Haggadah, "in every generation, every one of us is commanded to view him- or herself as if he or she came out of Egypt." Steinfels quotes Nathanson as bemoaning the fact that most of our contemporaries turn to popular culture to encounter these structures of meaning. In fact, Nathanson has helped us understand why Passover retains its power for most Jews and touches us as few other Jewish ritual moments do.

We Are Hagar

EVERY TORAH NARRATIVE must be read with close attention given to key words that relate the story to other biblical narratives. Nowhere is this principle more true than in the patriarchal narratives. Take the story of Hagar's banishment in Genesis 16. This is the first of two such accounts, the second one occurring in Genesis 21. The two accounts are similar in some respects, different in others.

In both, Sarah takes the initiative. But in this first account, Abraham is completely compliant: "Your maid is in your hands. Deal with her as you think right." In fact, the text does not explicitly tell us that Hagar was banished; rather, Sarah oppressed her and she fled. In the second, Abraham is distressed (Gen. 21:11), and it takes God's intervention to persuade him to banish Hagar and her son. Here, Abraham gives her bread and water before she leaves. In the first text, she leaves with nothing.

The difference between the two? Possibly, in the second instance, there is a son, Ishmael, who is involved. Abraham now has to contend with his feelings not only about Hagar, but also about his son. Hence his distress. Whatever he may feel about Hagar, he feels deeply about his son Ishmael.

Now look at some of the terms used in this first narrative. First, the name Hagar is clearly associated with the Hebrew word *ger,* "stranger," but she is identified as Egyptian. Also, note the three-fold reference to Hagar's being "oppressed" (Gen. 16:6–9 and 11). Now look at God's message to Abraham (Gen. 15:13): "Know that your offspring shall be strangers in a land not theirs, and they shall be enslaved and oppressed four hundred years."

The Hagar story, then, suggests the Israelite experience of Egyptian oppression. In fact, the connection is even closer. In this first account, we are not told where Hagar flees. However, in the second, we learn that she flees to the wilderness (Gen. 21:14), as did the Israelites, and she is desperate for water (Gen. 21:15), as were the Israelites. Finally, compare Genesis 16:11 and Exodus 2:24. In both cases, God is portrayed as "hearing" or "paying heed to" suffering, first of Hagar, and then of the Israelites. That is why Hagar is to call her son Ishmael, literally "God hears."

The second series of verbal associations connects the banishing of Hagar and Ishmael with the binding of Isaac in Genesis 22. Both deal with Abraham's relationship with a son, and in both the relationship is threatened. In both, Abraham rises early in the morning; in both, something is placed on someone's shoulder, in one case the water and bread on Hagar's shoulder, in the second the wood on Isaac's shoulder. In both, an angel appears to resolve the tension. Finally, both conclude with a reference to God's seeing. Hagar calls the God who appears to her "the God of seeing" (Gen. 16:13), and Abraham names the place where God appeared to him "the Lord will see" (Gen. 22:14).

The rabbinic tradition accentuates the connection between the two stories by having them read liturgically and successively on the two days of Rosh HaShanah. That is no accident; the two stories form one interconnected story. The binding of Isaac must be read against the backdrop of the banishment of Hagar and

Ishmael. The implicit message conveyed by these associations is not always clear. The Ishmael-Isaac association has led some to detect a totally subversive reading of the *Akedah,* the binding of Isaac.

In this reading, the binding of Isaac was retribution for the banishment of Ishmael. What God expected from Abraham, in both instances, was rebellion; that was the test. Because Abraham did not refuse to banish Ishmael, he was condemned to reenact the story with his other, apparently more beloved son as well.

In the case of the Hagar-Israelite set of associations, the message is equally subversive. Ostensibly, we are supposed to identify with Sarah and Isaac. But implicitly, our communal story, the story of the Israelites and later of the Jewish people, is modeled much more on Hagar and Ishmael than on Sarah and Isaac. Our story is also one of banishment, of wandering in wilderness of history, of vulnerability, of being near death, and of being rescued by God.

Hagar's ultimate vindication is in the midrash. After the *Akedah,* Sarah dies and Abraham marries a woman named Keturah (Gen. 25:1), who bears him many children. The midrash identifies Keturah with Hagar. Abraham wills all that he had to Isaac, gives his new sons gifts in his lifetime, and sends them "away from his son Isaac eastward" (Gen. 25:6). Then Abraham dies at a "good, ripe age, old and contented" (Gen. 25:8).

There are more questions than answers in this last stage of Abraham's life. Why does the midrash identify his new wife with Hagar? What does this tell us about Abraham's prior relation to Hagar? to Sarah? Why does he send his new sons away from Isaac? For Isaac's sake? To protect Isaac? For the sake of the new children? to spare them any association with Isaac's painful story? Yet Abraham dies contented!

We are also told that Ishmael and Isaac came together to bury Abraham. What did they talk about?

The Prophet and the Person

O N THE THREE SABBATHS leading to the solemn fast of Tisha
B'Av, we read prophetic "chapters of destruction," reflecting the traditional understanding that the Temple and Jerusalem
were destroyed because of Israel's sinfulness.

The first of these is the first chapter of Jeremiah, the haftarah
for *Parashat Pinchas*. The book of Jeremiah is fixed in the memory of those of us who studied it at the Jewish Theological Seminary with the late Professor Shalom Spiegel. Spiegel's course in
Jeremiah marked a high point in our rabbinical education. For
many of us, it was our introduction to the serious study of the
Prophets, and to this day we still recall many of his lectures
almost verbatim.

Why did Spiegel teach Jeremiah? Because of all of the
prophetic books, this is the most deeply personal. The book
intertwines classical prophetic utterances with the history of the
period, with anecdotal material about the prophet's personal
life, and even more with his innermost feelings about the events
he witnessed and about his prophetic calling. This intertwining

of the prophetic and the personal paralleled Spiegel's instructional style. He was never satisfied with our simply mastering the text itself—that was assumed from the outset. We had to memorize entire chapters of the book. But beyond this, it was clear that the text spoke to him in a deeply personal, existential way, and he was primarily concerned with allowing the material to speak to us, and through us to our students and congregants, in an equally personal way.

Jeremiah's name has been immortalized in our language with the term "jeremiad," defined as a lamentation. In fact, tradition ascribes the biblical book of Lamentations to his authorship. Much of his book is filled with anger and mourning over Israel's fate. But it also contains some of the most powerful expressions of hope and consolation, such as the concluding verse of our haftarah and chapter 31, which we read on the second day of Rosh HaShanah.

From the second verse of the first chapter of Jeremiah, we learn that Jeremiah began to prophesy in the year 625 BCE. He experienced the destruction of Jerusalem at the hands of the Babylonians.

Like Moses before him, Jeremiah strenuously resisted God's call to prophesy. That is evident in the first chapter and throughout the book. He curses the day he was born; he loathes the burden of loneliness and antagonism that his prophecies engendered. As mentioned above, he experienced the destruction of Jerusalem from a jail cell. He had been imprisoned as a traitor because he counseled submission to Babylonia; this was God's ordained punishment, and Israel had to bear it. Those were not popular words in a Jerusalem that was under siege.

But Jeremiah also insisted that Israel would survive Babylonia, that it would return and inhabit its land, and that once again, young men and women would be married in the cities of Judah and in the courtyards of Jerusalem (Jer. 33:10–11). Those words, recited to this day at every Jewish wedding, stand as an eternal prophecy of hope and Jewish continuity.

That tension between despair and hope, which pervades Jeremiah, is reflected in the final verse of our haftarah. Just where a haftarah was to begin and end was an arbitrary decision. The Rabbis could have ended our text with 1:19, the final verse of the first chapter. Instead they appended the first verses of chapter 2: God remembers "the devotion of your youth, your love as a bride, how you followed Me in the wilderness in a land not sown."

What a romanticized, idyllic portrait of Israel's early history! It hardly matches the biblical version of that period, which was in fact filled with Israel's constant rebellions against God. But Jeremiah's version of those years is what remains here, and despite the gloomy feel of the pre–Tisha B'Av weeks, that is what the Rabbis wish us to recall as well.

Redemption and Destruction

T HE CONVENTIONAL EXPLANATION for the name assigned to the Sabbath before Passover, Shabbat HaGadol, traces the name to the last verse of the haftarah for the day, taken from Malachi, chapter 3, which is also the final verse from the Prophets section of the *Tanakh:* "Lo, I will send the prophet Elijah to you before the coming of the awesome, fearful day of the Lord." The Hebrew for that "awesome" day is precisely *hagadol*.

But there is a decided ambiguity about these last verses. That very verse appears two verses earlier in our texts, and then is repeated after an intervening verse that reads: "He [Elijah] shall reconcile parents with children and children with parents, so that, when I come, I do not strike the whole land with utter destruction" (Mal. 3:24). The compilers of this material did not want the book to close with the theme of "utter destruction." Hence, they have us repeat the previous verse, which speaks of reconciliation.

The message, then, is a mixed one. Clearly the prophet is speaking about the events that will take place at the end of days, what theologians call eschatology. But he presents us with two contrasting scenarios for that day: One speaks of reconciliation, the other of utter destruction. So which is it? Probably one or the other, and it depends on us.

This ambiguity foreshadows a tension throughout later Jewish thought on this very topic. Two eschatological impulses emerge in this material. The first is optimistic; the second is deeply pessimistic. The first speaks of a gradually emerging, ever more perfect society, inspired throughout by the human impulse to seek reconciliation, to resolve the tensions that permeate our social structures. The second despairs that human beings of their own accord can achieve that reconciliation, and thus invokes God's appearance, at the very end of time as we know it, to destroy our familiar world, and, on its ruins, to build a perfect world.

Why this prophetic passage should be chosen for the Shabbat before Passover is clear. Passover is our festival of redemption, our historical deliverance from Egyptian bondage. But thoughts of this past redemption prompt us to dream of the ultimate redemption to come. This later, final deliverance will be universal, involving both nature and history, and it will be the ultimate one, the "end of days." The theme of redemption is everywhere in our Haggadah, most notably with the appearance of Elijah at our seder, for as Malachi tells us, Elijah is the herald of the messianic day.

These two eschatological impulses intertwine throughout Jewish intellectual history, one or the other becoming predominant at different times and in different societies. But clearly, today we are in the midst of a period where the pessimistic impulse is dominant. That impulse has been fueled by, among other factors, a persistent and pervasive despair about what human beings can accomplish on their own, and by a severe critique of the moral relativism that seems to be everywhere in our world.

To give one example, it is reflected in the anxiety that was felt by Israeli officials at the imminent approach of the year 2000 that some rabid, right-wing Christian messianic cults would visit Israel to celebrate the millennium and would cause all kinds of havoc. These groups derive their beliefs from their interpretation of books such as Daniel and, in Christian scripture, Revelation. There are also numerous references in the Prophets to this apocalyptic dimension of the "Day of the Lord" that speak of an ultimate cosmic war in which God will defeat the forces of evil forever.

This pessimistic impulse, especially when it is wed to a fundamentalist theology and political (even military) activism, is extremely dangerous. Witness the Branch Davidians, the Heaven's Gate cult, and the Jonestown massacre. All were eschatological cults that despaired of working creatively within society and sought to escape the world through a final, destructive act. The Israelis have much of which to be fearful.

Our world is complicated. The differences between good and evil are murky. It's not always easy to decide how we should act, how our society should conduct itself, how to make this world a better place for all of humanity. The message of Malachi is that the decision is in our hands. God waits for us. We can have reconciliation, or we can have utter destruction. That choice gives us plenty to think about as we approach our Passover. We should use this opportunity to dedicate ourselves to the task of repairing the world. The alternative does not bear thinking about.

The Dread of Time

MY EARLIEST ROSH HASHANAH MEMORY—indeed one of my earliest Jewish memories—is of standing next to my late father in the "old shul" (in contrast to the modernist "new shul," built in the 1940s) in the town where I was raised. The setting was awe inspiring, particularly to a five-year-old: a high-ceiling sanctuary, mahogany wall paneling, and red carpeting; the woman's gallery circling above us, the bimah in the center surrounded on four sides by long pews, and a carved mahogany gate opening to the three steps that led to the ark, garbed impressively on the High Holy Days in white and gold.

My community was too small to have a junior congregation, and in any case, my father would never have sent me. He believed that the place for me to learn about Jewish prayer was by standing next to and emulating him, not that he had much more of a Jewish education than I was having. But he was a "shul Jew" to his very last days. He may not have been able to translate the prayers, but he was a regular at the morning and evening minyan, enjoyed davening, and emerged from each service with a sense that all was right with his world. I trace my fascination with how prayer and liturgy work to his influence.

My Rosh HaShanah memory is the moment when we recite Unetaneh Tokef. To this day, it represents for me the very core of the Rosh HaShanah experience. This liturgical poem, dating probably from the geonic period, evokes the feeling of awe appropriate to the season by portraying a court scene. In this court, God is judge, prosecutor, and witness. The shofar sounds, angels tremble, the account books are open, and all creation passes before God in judgment.

And then: "On Rosh HaShanah it is written and on Yom Kippur it is sealed: ... Who shall live and who shall die." At that moment each year, I would look around to the group of elderly congregants in the sanctuary—*tallitot* draped over their heads, gently swaying, many in tears—and wonder, "Which of these men will be here next Rosh HaShanah? Which will be gone?"

I am now in a much different Jewish place than I was then. I understand that court scene as a vividly effective metaphor, so powerful that to this day, I react as I did when I was five. I may not believe that God literally "sits" in judgment, or that the account books are literally open. But I very much do believe that we are accountable for the lives we lead, and that this is the season of accountability.

Time and mortality are the core of the Rosh HaShanah experience. Time, because on Rosh HaShanah we become acutely sensitive to the passage of time. We say good-bye to the year that was and hello to the year that begins. Mortality, because, as Rabbi Abraham Joshua Heschel taught in his widely read book *The Sabbath*, we all suffer from a dread of time, and the dread of time is ultimately the dread of our death. There is much about our lives and our world that we can control, Rabbi Heschel taught, but we have absolutely no control over the passing of our individual time.

Rabbi Heschel used this notion of our dread of time to argue for an appreciation of Shabbat. But it applies even more to Rosh HaShanah. The Shabbat perspective is a week; the Rosh HaShanah perspective is a year. We live many weeks, but we live many fewer years. The message is now much sharper: Our time is limited, so we must treasure and shape the years allotted to us.

Rosh HaShanah remains the most enigmatic of our festivals. In the Bible, it is not even the first day of the year—that is the first of Nisan, in the spring. Apart from the sounding of the shofar, it has no distinctive biblical theme or texture. The Rosh HaShanah we observe today is the creation of postbiblical Judaism. It becomes the first day of the year, the anniversary of creation; under the spell of Yom Kippur ten days later, it inaugurates a period of introspection, self-evaluation, repentance, and renewal. This distinctive High Holy Days mood is sharpened by the sense of the preciousness of time, especially as we age.

Some may have caught the public television retrospective on the life and work of Leonard Bernstein. I found it fascinating, particularly when he confronts members of the Vienna Philharmonic Orchestra as they rehearse a symphony by Gustav Mahler. Mahler had converted to Christianity so he could be appointed conductor of the Vienna opera. But in the eyes of musical Vienna, he remained an outsider; his music was too "Semitic." The orchestra's hostility emerged in their playing of his score. Abruptly, Bernstein stops the rehearsal and speaks to the players, in German: "You've got all of the notes. But what's missing is Mahler. Mahler is nowhere to be found in your playing."

Much of what we will be doing over Rosh HaShanah is playing the notes: going to the synagogue, reciting the prayers, dipping an apple in honey, joining with our families. Notes are important; without them, there is no symphony. But just as the symphony is more than the notes, Rosh HaShanah is more than the synagogue, the prayers, and the honey. It is a reminder that our lives are fragile. We are like a fading flower, a passing shadow, a fugitive cloud, and a vanishing dream, the prayer says. It is a reminder that we are responsible for the lives we lead, and that the power to shape our lives is in our own hands.

Jacob Lives

"JACOB LIVED SEVENTEEN YEARS in the land of Egypt," begins the final scenes of the Joseph story and the concluding chapters of Genesis. But the reading in which it is found is called *Vayechi* because of its opening Hebrew word. The portion thus opens with a reference to life and to living, singularly interesting for a Torah reading that concludes with two dramatic death scenes— Jacob's and then Joseph's—and with a haftarah that describes still a third death scene, that of David.

This framing of the story has led to a spate of homilies on the polarities of life and death, and more specifically on how life transcends death. The burden of these homilies is that Jacob may have died, but in many ways he remains very much alive. For example, numerous eulogies on this theme followed the death in 1972 of our teacher Abraham Joshua Heschel, who died on this particular Sabbath.

At the very end of his life, Jacob is preoccupied with his imminent death and with how he will be recalled after he dies. He commands his sons to bury him in the land promised to his family and their progeny in Canaan, not in Egypt, in the very cave where his grandfather, grandmother, father, mother, and wife Leah were buried. Thus, he is almost literally "gathered to his people," the phrase the text uses for his dying (Gen. 49:33). He is to rejoin Abraham's progeny for eternity.

But Jacob contemplates his death on two earlier, far more desperate occasions. When he is told of Joseph's death at the hands of the brothers, he refuses to be comforted: "No, I will go down mourning to my son in Sheol" (Gen. 37:35). When the brothers ask to take Benjamin with them down to Egypt, he refuses: "If you take this one from me, too, and he meets with disaster, you will send my white head down to Sheol" (Gen. 44:29).

In the Bible, Sheol is the place where the dead go—the pit, the bowels of the earth, a place of worms and maggots. Jacob clearly believes that once he is in Sheol, he will not be able to communicate with his two dead sons. To be in Sheol is to be absolutely cut off from relationships, both with other people and with God, as it says in Psalm 6:6: "In Sheol, who can acclaim You?" The use of the term *sheol* for death here suggests that Jacob feared a tragic, premature death, a death that would leave significant relationships incomplete and his life without closure.

Such is how Jacob once envisioned his death. However, when he actually does die, he is "gathered to his people," the very epitome of relationship, and with them he will lie forever. The same phrase is used with Abraham's death (Gen. 25:8), and also with Isaac's (Gen. 35:29). This death concretizes and extends relationships to eternity; for now, of course, he has reconnected with both Joseph and Benjamin.

Jacob never contemplates any form of life after death. Notions such as the resurrection of the dead or the immortality of the soul are unknown at this stage in the development of biblical religion. Whatever immortality Jacob is to enjoy rests in his association with kin, his family and his people. That includes us, for every year we return to and read anew the story of Jacob and his extended family, their adventures, their intrigues, their fears, and their dreams. Jacob's immortality is assured through the bonds of our communal memory. How many great men and women of antiquity can claim to enjoy that kind of immortality?

Indeed, the first word of this Torah reading is absolutely true. Jacob lives on and will continue to live among us as long as we continue to recall his presence.

Interim Eschatologies

THE SABBATH BETWEEN ROSH HASHANAH and Yom Kippur is called Shabbat Shuvah, the Sabbath of Return, after the opening words of its haftarah, *Shuvah Yisrael*, "Return O Israel."

Unique among the *haftarot*, this one draws from the writings of three prophets: Hosea (14:2–10), Micah (7:18–20), and Joel (2:15–27). The ensemble is a classic Jewish statement regarding the power of *teshuvah* (repentance), God's eternal compassion and readiness to accept our repentance, and the blessings that are surely to flow when we do return.

That *teshuvah* has the power to erase our sins and preempt God's punishment is a stunning contribution from the Prophets. Deuteronomy (30:1–3) teaches that if we would return to God after having been punished, God will surely redeem us. But the notion that God waits patiently for us to repent before determining our fate originated with the Prophets, and thereafter became central to Judaism.

In fact, the midrash claims that repentance was created even before the creation of the world. God seems to have realized that the world could simply not endure unless, inherent in the very nature of things, was the infinite possibility for us to turn our lives around. Nothing is sealed, no gates are closed; our lives are in our hands to shape as we wish. That claim is an explicit rejection of the power of fate or predestination, of the notion that we have to be just the way we are. It is a remarkable statement of faith in human beings and in our potential for regeneration.

Every moment of our lives is ripe for *teshuvah*. But our tradition also provides us with windows of opportunity. There are moments or seasons when our liturgy and ritual combine to raise our consciousness and place our responsibility for self-assessment on our immediate agenda. This ten-day period is the most eminent of those windows. It culminates when Yom Kippur draws to a close with the N'ilah service. That moment has a distinctive feel of its own: Yom Kippur and our *teshuvah* have done their work. As Micah said, "Our sins have been hurled into the depths of the sea. We are as newborns again" (Mic. 7:19).

This is one of those moments, scattered through the year, when we are privileged to taste, however fleetingly, what it would be like to live a perfect life in a perfect world. Shabbat is another one of those moments—it is called *me'ein olam haba*, a taste of the age-to-come. Still another such moment is the climax of the wedding service, when Jeremiah's words remind us that the song of the bridegroom and bride is one of our most powerful affirmations of hope for redemption.

These moments are fleeting and evanescent: Shabbat ends with the Havdalah service, which wrenches us back into the working week; the wedding ends with the breaking of the glass, reminding us that our world is still not redeemed. Immediately after the close of Yom Kippur, we recite the familiar daily Ma'ariv service, which begins with the words "And God, being merciful, grants atonement for sin."

Atonement for sin? Immediately after the close of Yom Kippur? Of course, Rabbi Abraham Joshua Heschel taught us, for how do we know that our repentance was pure and sincere?

We call these fleeting anticipations of life and of the world perfected "interim eschatologies." Eschatology is the part of theology that deals with the end of days, the messianic age. I first heard the notion of an interim eschatology from my teacher, Professor Gerson Cohen, the former Chancellor of the Jewish Theological Seminary. Cohen was obsessed with the importance of Jewish eschatology. Every significant Jewish movement, he taught, had an eschatological thrust, and he bemoaned the reluctance of all but the most extreme right-wing Jewish movements of our age to teach classical Jewish eschatological themes.

But Cohen also recognized that on this issue, Judaism puts us in a bind. On one hand, eschatology is omnipresent in our liturgy. Wherever we turn, we find references to the coming of the Messiah, the return to Zion, the rebuilding of the Temple, the restoration of the Temple ritual, God's final judgment on all human strivings, the resurrection of the dead, and the emergence of an age of universal peace and justice. On the other hand, Judaism cautions us again and again against attempting to calculate when the end will come, against aggressively forcing God's hand, and against being overly quick to interpret historical events as part of a messianic scenario.

This caution was bred out of our people's painful historical experience with the potentially anarchic power of overtly messianic movements, of which Christianity and Sabbateanism were the most dramatic instances. Thus, a tragic dialectic entered into our lives as Jews. Pray for the Messiah daily, but don't do anything—apart from the daily, normative demands of Torah— to hasten the Messiah's coming. "If he delays, wait for him," says Maimonides, echoing Habakkuk (2:3).

To ease the dilemma, Gerson Cohen taught, we have these interim eschatological moments—fleeting anticipations of what it will be like when the Messiah does come. These moments serve as a release for the buildup of our messianic fervor. They remind us that however chaotic today may seem, chaos will not have the last word. As there was cosmos at the beginning, so will there be cosmos at the end. In the meantime, Shabbat, Yom Kippur, and weddings provide us with a taste of what that true redemption will be like. Now, let us wait for the day that will be the eternal Shabbat!

A Drama of Life
and Death

MANY OF US MAY REMEMBER seeing meat being kashered in the kitchens of our childhood homes. The raw meat was soaked, salted, placed on wooden drain boards so that the blood would drain, and then rinsed. Today, all of this is done behind the scenes by kosher butchers, thereby depriving our families of a significant Jewish educational experience.

This ritual kashering fulfills an injunction that appears twice in the Torah portion *Re'eh*. In Deuteronomy 12:16 and again in verses 23–25, we are forbidden to consume the blood of animals we have slaughtered. In the latter text, the Torah adds a brief explanation: We must not consume the blood, "for the blood is the life and you must not consume the life with the flesh." Instead, we are to "pour it out on the ground like water." We may not pour out the blood ourselves, but we do drain it.

This injunction appears also in Leviticus 17:10–11, where again we are told, "for the life of the flesh is in the blood." And in Genesis 9:4, in the injunctions delivered to the sons of Noah, a similar text reads, "You must not, however, eat the flesh with its life-blood in it."

In all of these cases, the Hebrew word for "life" is *nefesh*. This Hebrew term is at the heart of a central Jewish theological doctrine with an interesting history.

In the postbiblical tradition, three terms are typically used to designate what we call "soul": *ruach, nefesh,* and *neshamah.* Kabbalists make fine distinctions among these three terms, but they are largely interchangeable. They all share the notion that what we call the soul is a distinct entity, separate from the body. The soul enters the body at birth, or in some traditions at conception. It exists within the body during our lifetime, and then separates from the body at death. This view, which originated in Greek philosophy, is dualistic: Body and soul are two distinct entities. It is but one of the many Hellenistic influences on Judaism.

But the Bible itself knows nothing of this dualistic view of the human person. The classic text on the issue is Genesis 2:7. "The Lord God formed man [in Hebrew, *adam,* which is translated "man" here because the woman is created later in the chapter] from the dust of the earth. He blew into his nostrils the breath of life, and man became a living being." God did not introduce a distinct, separate entity into the clod of earth dust. Rather, God vivified the clod of dust.

In teaching this text, I use the homely example of what happens when our car battery dies. We connect our battery to a "living" battery that sparks the dead battery into life. This divine "spark" is what vivified the dust. When we die, the spark is extinguished. It doesn't go anywhere; it is simply extinguished.

Only in the later tradition does this "breath of life" become a "soul" that survives the body at death and returns to God, who created it. According to this doctrine, at the end of days, this soul is reunited with its now resurrected body, and the human person, reconstituted as during his or her lifetime, comes before God in judgment.

But in *Parashat Re'eh,* the term *nefesh* is quite properly translated as "life." In a more extended sense, it signifies a living human being, or simply a person. In the opening verses of Exodus, for example, we are told that "the total number of persons that were of Jacob's issue" who came to Egypt were seventy (Ex. 1:5), and the Hebrew word here for "persons" again is *nefesh.* Seventy people went to Egypt, not seventy disembodied souls.

The same development occurs with the word *neshamah.* In the postbiblical tradition up to and including our own day, it has come to mean "soul." In the Bible, it simply means a living, breathing person. The very last verse of the very last psalm (Ps. 150:6), which uses the Hebrew phrase *kol haneshamah,* does not mean "Let all souls praise the Lord," but rather, "Let all living beings praise the Lord," or as the Jewish Publication Society translates, "Let all that breathes praise the Lord."

In both of these instances, the Bible recognizes that the sources of life are blood and breath. Lose one of them and life ceases. To consume an animal's blood, then, is tantamount to consuming the life of the animal. That we must not do, for life is sacred. When, years ago, we used to see the blood draining from the meat on our kashering drain boards, we were not simply observing a quaint ritual. What was being symbolically enacted, then, was nothing less than a drama of life and death.

Suggestions for Further Reading

Blumenthal, David R. *Facing the Abusing God: A Theology of Protest.* Louisville, Ky.: Westminster John Knox Press, 1993.

Buber, Martin. *I and Thou.* New York: Charles Scribner's Sons, 1970.

Dorff, Elliot N. *Knowing God: Jewish Journeys to the Unknowable.* Northvale, N.J.: Jason Aronson, 1996.

———. *The Unfolding Tradition: Jewish Law After Sinai.* New York: Aviv Press, 2005.

Fackenheim, Emil L. *Quest for Past and Future: Essays in Jewish Theology.* Bloomington: Indiana University Press, 1968.

Geller, Stephen A. *Sacred Enigmas: Literary Religion in the Hebrew Bible.* New York: Routledge, 1996.

Gillman, Neil. *The Death of Death: Resurrection and Immortality in Jewish Thought.* Woodstock, Vt.: Jewish Lights Publishing, 2000.

———. *The Way Into Encountering God in Judaism.* Woodstock, Vt.: Jewish Lights Publishing, 2004.

Goldberg, Harvey E. *Jewish Passages: Cycles of Jewish Life*: Berkeley: University of California Press, 2003

Green, Rabbi Arthur. *Seek My Face: A Jewish Mystical Theology.* Woodstock, Vt.: Jewish Lights Publishing, 2003.

Heilman, Samuel, ed., *Death Bereavement and Mourning.* Piscataway, N.J.: Transaction Publishers, 2005.

Herberg, Will. *Judaism and Modern Man: An Interpretation of Jewish Religion.* Woodstock, Vt.: Jewish Lights Publishing, 1997.

Heschel, Abraham Joshua. *God in Search of Man: A Philosophy of Judaism*. Philadelphia: Jewish Publication Society, 1956.

———. *Heavenly Torah as Refracted Through the Generations*. New York: Continuum, 2005.

———. *A Passion for Truth*. Woodstock, Vt.: Jewish Lights Publishing, 1995.

———. *The Prophets*. Philadelphia: Jewish Publication Society, 1962.

Hoffman, Rabbi Lawrence A., ed. *My People's Prayer Book: Traditional Prayers, Modern Commentaries*, vols. 1–10. Woodstock, Vt.: Jewish Lights Publishing, 1997–2006.

Levenson, Jon D. *Creation and the Persistence of Evil: The Jewish Drama of Divine Omnipotence*. Princeton, N.J.: Princeton University Press, 1994.

McFague, Sallie. *Metaphorical Theology: Models of God in Religious Language*. Philadelphia: Fortress Press, 1997.

Miles, Jack. *God: A Biography*. New York: Vintage, 1996.

Muffs, Yochanan. *Love and Joy: Law, Language and Religion in Ancient Israel*. New York: The Jewish Theological Seminary of America, 1992.

———. *The Personhood of God: Biblical Theology, Human Faith and the Divine Image*. Woodstock, Vt.: Jewish Lights Publishing, 2005.

Twersky, Isadore, ed. *A Maimonides Reader*. West Orange, N.J.: Behrman House, 1976.

Index of Torah Readings

Inspiration

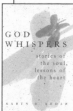

God in All Moments
Mystical & Practical Spiritual Wisdom from Hasidic Masters
Edited and translated by Or N. Rose with Ebn D. Leader

Hasidic teachings on how to be mindful in religious practice and cultivating every-day ethical behavior—*hanhagot*. 5½ x 8½, 192 pp, Quality PB, ISBN 1-58023-186-1 **$16.95**

Our Dance with God: Finding Prayer, Perspective and Meaning in the Stories of Our Lives *By Karyn D. Kedar*

Inspiring spiritual insight to guide you on your life journeys and teach you to live and thrive in two conflicting worlds: the rational/material and the spiritual.
6 x 9, 176 pp, Quality PB, ISBN 1-58023-202-7 **$16.99**

Also Available: **The Dance of the Dolphin** (Hardcover edition of *Our Dance with God*)
6 x 9, 176 pp, Hardcover, ISBN 1-58023-154-3 **$19.95**

The Empty Chair: Finding Hope and Joy—Timeless Wisdom from a Hasidic Master, Rebbe Nachman of Breslov *Adapted by Moshe Mykoff and the Breslov Research Institute*
4 x 6, 128 pp, 2-color text, Deluxe PB w/flaps, ISBN 1-879045-67-2 **$9.95**

The Gentle Weapon: Prayers for Everyday and Not-So-Everyday Moments—Timeless Wisdom from the Teachings of the Hasidic Master, Rebbe Nachman of Breslov
Adapted by Moshe Mykoff and S. C. Mizrahi, together with the Breslov Research Institute
4 x 6, 144 pp, 2-color text, Deluxe PB w/flaps, ISBN 1-58023-022-9 **$9.95**

God Whispers: Stories of the Soul, Lessons of the Heart *By Karyn D. Kedar*
6 x 9, 176 pp, Quality PB, ISBN 1-58023-088-1 **$15.95**

An Orphan in History: One Man's Triumphant Search for His Jewish Roots
By Paul Cowan. Afterword by Rachel Cowan. 6 x 9, 288 pp, Quality PB, ISBN 1-58023-135-7 **$16.95**

Restful Reflections: Nighttime Inspiration to Calm the Soul, Based on Jewish Wisdom
By Rabbi Kerry M. Olitzky & Rabbi Lori Forman 4½ x 6½, 448 pp, Quality PB, ISBN 1-58023-091-1 **$15.95**

Sacred Intentions: Daily Inspiration to Strengthen the Spirit, Based on Jewish Wisdom
By Rabbi Kerry M. Olitzky and Rabbi Lori Forman 4½ x 6½, 448 pp, Quality PB, ISBN 1-58023-061-X **$15.95**

Kabbalah/Mysticism/Enneagram

Awakening to Kabbalah: The Guiding Light of Spiritual Fulfillment
By Rav Michael Laitman, PhD

A distinctive, personal and awe-filled introduction to this ancient wisdom tradition.
6 x 9, 192 pp, Hardcover, ISBN 1-58023-264-7 **$21.99**

Seek My Face: A Jewish Mystical Theology
By Dr. Arthur Green

This classic work of contemporary Jewish theology, revised and updated, is a profound, deeply personal statement of the lasting truths of Jewish mysticism and the basic faith claims of Judaism. 6 x 9, 304 pp, Quality PB, ISBN 1-58023-130-6 **$19.95**

Zohar: Annotated & Explained
Translation and annotation by Dr. Daniel C. Matt. Foreword by Andrew Harvey

Offers insightful yet unobtrusive commentary to the masterpiece of Jewish mysticism. 5½ x 8½, 160 pp, Quality PB, ISBN 1-893361-51-9 **$15.99** *(A SkyLight Paths book)*

Cast in God's Image: Discover Your Personality Type Using the Enneagram and Kabbalah
By Rabbi Howard A. Addison
7 x 9, 176 pp, Quality PB, Layflat binding, 20+ journaling exercises, ISBN 1-58023-124-1 **$16.95**

Ehyeh: A Kabbalah for Tomorrow *By Dr. Arthur Green*
6 x 9, 224 pp, Quality PB, ISBN 1-58023-213-2 **$16.99**; Hardcover, ISBN 1-58023-125-X **$21.95**

The Enneagram and Kabbalah, 2nd Edition: Reading Your Soul
By Rabbi Howard A. Addison 6 x 9, 192 pp, Quality PB, ISBN 1-58023-229-9 **$16.99**

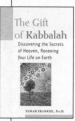

Finding Joy: A Practical Spiritual Guide to Happiness *By Dannel I. Schwartz with Mark Hass*
6 x 9, 192 pp, Quality PB, ISBN 1-58023-009-1 **$14.95**

The Gift of Kabbalah: Discovering the Secrets of Heaven, Renewing Your Life on Earth
By Tamar Frankiel, Ph.D.
6 x 9, 256 pp, Quality PB, ISBN 1-58023-141-1 **$16.95**; Hardcover, ISBN 1-58023-108-X **$21.95**

The Way Into Jewish Mystical Tradition *By Lawrence Kushner*
6 x 9, 224 pp, Quality PB, ISBN 1-58023-200-0 **$18.99**; Hardcover, ISBN 1-58023-029-6 **$21.95**

Holidays/Holy Days

Yom Kippur Readings: Inspiration, Information and Contemplation
Edited by Rabbi Dov Peretz Elkins with section introductions from Arthur Green's These Are the Words
An extraordinary collection of readings, prayers and insights that enable the modern worshiper to enter into the spirit of the Day of Atonement in a personal and powerful way, permitting the meaning of Yom Kippur to enter the heart.
6 x 9, 348 pp, Hardcover, ISBN 1-58023-271-X **$24.99**

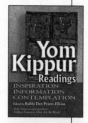

Leading the Passover Journey
The Seder's Meaning Revealed, the Haggadah's Story Retold
By Rabbi Nathan Laufer
Uncovers the hidden meaning of the Seder's rituals and customs
6 x 9, 208 pp, Hardcover, ISBN 1-58023-211-6 **$24.99**

Reclaiming Judaism as a Spiritual Practice: Holy Days and Shabbat
By Rabbi Goldie Milgram
Provides a framework for understanding the powerful and often unexplained intellectual, emotional, and spiritual tools that are essential for a lively, relevant, and fulfilling Jewish spiritual practice. 7 x 9, 272 pp, Quality PB, ISBN 1-58023-205-1 **$19.99**

7th Heaven: Celebrating Shabbat with Rebbe Nachman of Breslov
By Moshe Mykoff with the Breslov Research Institute
Explores the art of consciously observing Shabbat and understanding in-depth many of the day's spiritual practices. 5⅛ x 8¼, 224 pp, Deluxe PB w/flaps, ISBN 1-58023-175-6 **$18.95**

The Women's Passover Companion
Women's Reflections on the Festival of Freedom
Edited by Rabbi Sharon Cohen Anisfeld, Tara Mohr, and Catherine Spector
Groundbreaking. A provocative conversation about women's relationships to Passover as well as the roots and meanings of women's seders.
6 x 9, 352 pp, Hardcover, ISBN 1-58023-128-4 **$24.95**

The Women's Seder Sourcebook
Rituals & Readings for Use at the Passover Seder
Edited by Rabbi Sharon Cohen Anisfeld, Tara Mohr, and Catherine Spector
Gathers the voices of more than one hundred women in readings, personal and creative reflections, commentaries, blessings, and ritual suggestions that can be incorporated into your Passover celebration.
6 x 9, 384 pp, Hardcover, ISBN 1-58023-136-5 **$24.95**

Creating Lively Passover Seders: A Sourcebook of Engaging Tales, Texts & Activities
By David Arnow, Ph.D. 7 x 9, 416 pp, Quality PB, ISBN 1-58023-184-5 **$24.99**

Hanukkah, 2nd Edition: The Family Guide to Spiritual Celebration
By Dr. Ron Wolfson. Edited by Joel Lurie Grishaver.
7 x 9, 240 pp, illus., Quality PB, ISBN 1-58023-122-5 **$18.95**

The Jewish Family Fun Book: Holiday Projects, Everyday Activities, and Travel Ideas with Jewish Themes *By Danielle Dardashti and Roni Sarig. Illus. by Avi Katz.*
6 x 9, 288 pp, 70+ b/w illus. & diagrams, Quality PB, ISBN 1-58023-171-3 **$18.95**

The Jewish Gardening Cookbook: Growing Plants & Cooking for Holidays & Festivals *By Michael Brown* 6 x 9, 224 pp, 30+ illus., Quality PB, ISBN 1-58023-116-0 **$16.95**

The Jewish Lights Book of Fun Classroom Activities: Simple and Seasonal Projects for Teachers and Students *By Danielle Dardashti and Roni Sarig*
6 x 9, 240 pp, Quality PB, ISBN 1–58023–206–X **$19.99**

Passover, 2nd Edition: The Family Guide to Spiritual Celebration
By Dr. Ron Wolfson with Joel Lurie Grishaver 7 x 9, 352 pp, Quality PB, ISBN 1-58023-174-8 **$19.95**

Shabbat, 2nd Edition: The Family Guide to Preparing for and Celebrating the Sabbath
By Dr. Ron Wolfson 7 x 9, 320 pp, illus., Quality PB, ISBN 1-58023-164-0 **$19.95**

Sharing Blessings: Children's Stories for Exploring the Spirit of the Jewish Holidays
By Rahel Musleah and Michael Klayman
8½ x 11, 64 pp, Full-color illus., Hardcover, ISBN 1-879045-71-0 **$18.95** *For ages 6 & up*

Life Cycle
Marriage / Parenting / Family / Aging

Jewish Fathers: A Legacy of Love
Photographs by Lloyd Wolf. Essays by Paula Wolfson. Foreword by Harold S. Kushner.
Honors the role of contemporary Jewish fathers in America. Each father tells in his own words what it means to be a parent and Jewish, and what he learned from his own father. Insightful photos. 9½ x 9⅞, 144 pp with 100+ duotone photos, Hardcover, ISBN 1-58023-204-3 **$30.00**

The New Jewish Baby Album: Creating and Celebrating the Beginning of a Spiritual Life—A Jewish Lights Companion
By the Editors at Jewish Lights. Foreword by Anita Diamant. Preface by Sandy Eisenberg Sasso.
A spiritual keepsake that will be treasured for generations. More than just a memory book, *shows you how—and why it's important*—to create a Jewish home and a Jewish life. 8 x 10, 64 pp, Deluxe Padded Hardcover, Full-color illus., ISBN 1-58023-138-1 **$19.95**

The Jewish Pregnancy Book: A Resource for the Soul, Body & Mind during Pregnancy, Birth & the First Three Months
By Sandy Falk, M.D., and Rabbi Daniel Judson, with Steven A. Rapp
Includes medical information, prayers and rituals for each stage of pregnancy, from a liberal Jewish perspective. 7 x 10, 208 pp, Quality PB, b/w illus., ISBN 1-58023-178-0 **$16.95**

Celebrating Your New Jewish Daughter: Creating Jewish Ways to Welcome Baby Girls into the Covenant—New and Traditional Ceremonies
By Debra Nussbaum Cohen 6 x 9, 272 pp, Quality PB, ISBN 1-58023-090-3 **$18.95**

The New Jewish Baby Book, 2nd Edition: Names, Ceremonies & Customs—A Guide for Today's Families *By Anita Diamant* 6 x 9, 336 pp, Quality PB, ISBN 1-58023-251-5 **$19.99**

Parenting As a Spiritual Journey: Deepening Ordinary and Extraordinary Events into Sacred Occasions *By Rabbi Nancy Fuchs-Kreimer* 6 x 9, 224 pp, Quality PB, ISBN 1-58023-016-4 **$16.95**

Judaism for Two: A Spiritual Guide for Strengthening and Celebrating Your Loving Relationship *By Rabbi Nancy Fuchs-Kreimer and Rabbi Nancy H. Wiener*
Addresses the ways Jewish teachings can enhance and strengthen committed relationships. 6 x 9, 208 pp, Quality PB, ISBN 1-58023-254-X **$16.99**

Embracing the Covenant: Converts to Judaism Talk About Why & How
By Rabbi Allan Berkowitz and Patti Moskovitz 6 x 9, 192 pp, Quality PB, ISBN 1-879045-50-8 **$16.95**

The Guide to Jewish Interfaith Family Life: An InterfaithFamily.com Handbook
Edited by Ronnie Friedland and Edmund Case 6 x 9, 384 pp, Quality PB, ISBN 1-58023-153-5 **$18.95**

Introducing My Faith and My Community
The Jewish Outreach Institute Guide for the Christian in a Jewish Interfaith Relationship
By Rabbi Kerry M. Olitzky 6 x 9, 176 pp, Quality PB, ISBN 1-58023-192-6 **$16.99**

Making a Successful Jewish Interfaith Marriage: The Jewish Outreach Institute Guide to Opportunities, Challenges and Resources
By Rabbi Kerry M. Olitzky with Joan Peterson Littman 6 x 9, 176 pp, Quality PB, ISBN 1-58023-170-5 **$16.95**

The Creative Jewish Wedding Book: A Hands-On Guide to New & Old Traditions, Ceremonies & Celebrations *By Gabrielle Kaplan-Mayer*
Provides the tools to create the most meaningful Jewish traditional or alternative wedding by using ritual elements to express your unique style and spirituality. 9 x 9, 288 pp, b/w photos, Quality PB, ISBN 1-58023-194-2 **$19.99**

Divorce Is a Mitzvah: A Practical Guide to Finding Wholeness and Holiness When Your Marriage Dies *By Rabbi Perry Netter. Afterword by Rabbi Laura Geller.*
6 x 9, 224 pp, Quality PB, ISBN 1-58023-172-1 **$16.95**

A Heart of Wisdom: Making the Jewish Journey from Midlife through the Elder Years
Edited by Susan Berrin. Foreword by Harold Kushner. 6 x 9, 384 pp, Quality PB, ISBN 1-58023-051-2 **$18.95**

So That Your Values Live On: Ethical Wills and How to Prepare Them
Edited by Jack Riemer and Nathaniel Stampfer 6 x 9, 272 pp, Quality PB, ISBN 1-879045-34-6 **$18.95**

Spirituality

Does the Soul Survive? A Jewish Journey to Belief in Afterlife, Past Lives & Living with Purpose *By Rabbi Elie Kaplan Spitz. Foreword by Brian L Weiss, M.D.*
Spitz relates his own experiences and those shared with him by people he has worked with as a rabbi, and shows us that belief in afterlife and past lives, so often approached with reluctance, is in fact true to Jewish tradition.
6 x 9, 288 pp, Quality PB, ISBN 1-58023-165-9 **$16.95**; Hardcover, ISBN 1-58023-094-6 **$21.95**

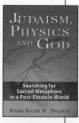

First Steps to a New Jewish Spirit: Reb Zalman's Guide to Recapturing the Intimacy & Ecstasy in Your Relationship with God
By Rabbi Zalman M. Schachter-Shalomi with Donald Gropman
An extraordinary spiritual handbook that restores psychic and physical vigor by introducing us to new models and alternative ways of practicing Judaism. Offers meditation and contemplation exercises for enriching the most important aspects of everyday life. 6 x 9, 144 pp, Quality PB, ISBN 1-58023-182-9 **$16.95**

God in Our Relationships: Spirituality between People from the Teachings of Martin Buber *By Rabbi Dennis S. Ross*
On the eightieth anniversary of Buber's classic work, we can discover new answers to critical issues in our lives. Inspiring examples from Ross's own life—as congregational rabbi, father, hospital chaplain, social worker, and husband—illustrate Buber's difficult-to-understand ideas about how we encounter God and each other. 5½ x 8½, 160 pp, Quality PB, ISBN 1-58023-147-0 **$16.95**

Judaism, Physics and God: Searching for Sacred Metaphors in a Post-Einstein World *By Rabbi David W. Nelson*
In clear, non-technical terms, this provocative fusion of religion and science examines the great theories of modern physics to find new ways for contemporary people to express their spiritual beliefs and thoughts.
6 x 9, 352 pp, Hardcover, ISBN 1-58023-252-3 **$24.99**

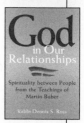

The Jewish Lights Spirituality Handbook: A Guide to Understanding, Exploring & Living a Spiritual Life *Edited by Stuart M. Matlins*
What exactly is "Jewish" about spirituality? How do I make it a part of my life? Fifty of today's foremost spiritual leaders share their ideas and experience with us.
6 x 9, 456 pp, Quality PB, ISBN 1-58023-093-8 **$19.95**; Hardcover, ISBN 1-58023-100-4 **$24.95**

Bringing the Psalms to Life: How to Understand and Use the Book of Psalms
By Dr. Daniel F. Polish
6 x 9, 208 pp, Quality PB, ISBN 1-58023-157-8 **$16.95**; Hardcover, ISBN 1-58023-077-6 **$21.95**

God & the Big Bang: Discovering Harmony between Science & Spirituality
By Dr. Daniel C. Matt 6 x 9, 216 pp, Quality PB, ISBN 1-879045-89-3 **$16.95**

Godwrestling—Round 2: Ancient Wisdom, Future Paths
By Rabbi Arthur Waskow 6 x 9, 352 pp, Quality PB, ISBN 1-879045-72-9 **$18.95**

One God Clapping: The Spiritual Path of a Zen Rabbi *By Rabbi Alan Lew with Sherril Jaffe*
5½ x 8½, 336 pp, Quality PB, ISBN 1-58023-115-2 **$16.95**

The Path of Blessing: Experiencing the Energy and Abundance of the Divine
By Rabbi Marcia Prager 5½ x 8½, 240 pp., Quality PB, ISBN 1-58023-148-9 **$16.95**

Six Jewish Spiritual Paths: A Rationalist Looks at Spirituality *By Rabbi Rifat Sonsino*
6 x 9, 208 pp, Quality PB, ISBN 1-58023-167-5 **$16.95**; Hardcover, ISBN 1-58023-095-4 **$21.95**

Soul Judaism: Dancing with God into a New Era
By Rabbi Wayne Dosick 5½ x 8½, 304 pp, Quality PB, ISBN 1-58023-053-9 **$16.95**

Stepping Stones to Jewish Spiritual Living: Walking the Path Morning, Noon, and Night *By Rabbi James L Mirel and Karen Bonnell Werth*
6 x 9, 240 pp, Quality PB, ISBN 1-58023-074-1 **$16.95**; Hardcover, ISBN 1-58023-003-2 **$21.95**

There Is No Messiah ... and You're It: The Stunning Transformation of Judaism's Most Provocative Idea *By Rabbi Robert N. Levine, D.D.*
6 x 9, 192 pp, Quality PB, ISBN 1-58023-255-8 **$16.95**; Hardcover, ISBN 1-58023-173-X **$21.95**

These Are the Words: A Vocabulary of Jewish Spiritual Life *By Dr. Arthur Green*
6 x 9, 304 pp, Quality PB, ISBN 1-58023-107-1 **$18.95**

Spirituality/Women's Interest

The Quotable Jewish Woman: Wisdom, Inspiration & Humor from the Mind & Heart *Edited and compiled by Elaine Bernstein Partnow*
The definitive collection of ideas, reflections, humor, and wit of over 300 Jewish women.
6 x 9, 496 pp, Hardcover, ISBN 1-58023-193-4 **$29.99**

Lifecycles, Vol. 1: Jewish Women on Life Passages & Personal Milestones
Edited and with introductions by Rabbi Debra Orenstein 6 x 9, 480 pp, Quality PB, ISBN 1-58023-018-0 **$19.95**

Lifecycles, Vol. 2: Jewish Women on Biblical Themes in Contemporary Life
Edited and with introductions by Rabbi Debra Orenstein and Rabbi Jane Rachel Litman
6 x 9, 464 pp, Quality PB, ISBN 1-58023-019-9 **$19.95**

Moonbeams: A Hadassah Rosh Hodesh Guide *Edited by Carol Diament, Ph.D.*
8½ x 11, 240 pp, Quality PB, ISBN 1-58023-099-7 **$20.00**

ReVisions: Seeing Torah through a Feminist Lens *By Rabbi Elyse Goldstein*
5½ x 8½, 224 pp, Quality PB, ISBN 1-58023-117-9 **$16.95**

White Fire: A Portrait of Women Spiritual Leaders in America
By Rabbi Malka Drucker. Photographs by Gay Block.
7 x 10, 320 pp, 30+ b/w photos, Hardcover, ISBN 1-893361-64-0 **$24.95** *(A SkyLight Paths book)*

Women of the Wall: Claiming Sacred Ground at Judaism's Holy Site
Edited by Phyllis Chesler and Rivka Haut 6 x 9, 496 pp, b/w photos, Hardcover, ISBN 1-58023-161-6 **$34.95**

The Women's Haftarah Commentary: New Insights from Women Rabbis on the 54 Weekly Haftarah Portions, the 5 Megillot & Special Shabbatot
Edited by Rabbi Elyse Goldstein 6 x 9, 560 pp, Hardcover, ISBN 1-58023-133-0 **$39.99**

The Women's Torah Commentary: New Insights from Women Rabbis on the 54 Weekly Torah Portions *Edited by Rabbi Elyse Goldstein*
6 x 9, 496 pp, Hardcover, ISBN 1-58023-076-8 **$34.95**

The Year Mom Got Religion: One Woman's Midlife Journey into Judaism
By Lee Meyerhoff Hendler 6 x 9, 208 pp, Quality PB, ISBN 1-58023-070-9 **$15.95**

See Holidays for *The Women's Passover Companion: Women's Reflections on the Festival of Freedom* and *The Women's Seder Sourcebook: Rituals & Readings for Use at the Passover Seder*. Also see Bar/Bat Mitzvah for *The JGirl's Guide: The Young Jewish Woman's Handbook for Coming of Age.*

Travel

Israel—A Spiritual Travel Guide, 2nd Edition
A Companion for the Modern Jewish Pilgrim
By Rabbi Lawrence A. Hoffman 4¾ x 10, 256 pp, Quality PB, illus., ISBN 1-58023-261-2 **$18.99**
Also Available: **The Israel Mission Leader's Guide** ISBN 1-58023-085-7 **$4.95**

12 Steps

100 Blessings Every Day Daily Twelve Step Recovery Affirmations, Exercises for Personal Growth & Renewal Reflecting Seasons of the Jewish Year
By Rabbi Kerry M. Olitzky. Foreword by Rabbi Neil Gillman.
One-day-at-a-time monthly format. Reflects on the rhythm of the Jewish calendar to bring insight to recovery from addictions.
4½ x 6¼, 432 pp, Quality PB, ISBN 1-879045-30-3 **$15.99**

Recovery from Codependence: A Jewish Twelve Steps Guide to Healing Your Soul
By Rabbi Kerry M. Olitzky 6 x 9, 160 pp, Quality PB, ISBN 1-879045-32-X **$13.95**

Renewed Each Day: Daily Twelve Step Recovery Meditations Based on the Bible
By Rabbi Kerry M. Olitzky and Aaron Z.
Vol. 1—Genesis & Exodus: 6 x 9, 224 pp, Quality PB, ISBN 1-879045-12-5 **$14.95**
Vol. 2—Leviticus, Numbers & Deuteronomy: 6 x 9, 280 pp, Quality PB, ISBN 1-879045-13-3 **$18.99**

Twelve Jewish Steps to Recovery: A Personal Guide to Turning from Alcoholism & Other Addictions—Drugs, Food, Gambling, Sex...
By Rabbi Kerry M. Olitzky and Stuart A. Copans, M.D. Preface by Abraham J. Twerski, M.D.
6 x 9, 144 pp, Quality PB, ISBN 1-879045-09-5 **$14.95**

Spirituality/Lawrence Kushner

Filling Words with Light: Hasidic and Mystical Reflections on Jewish Prayer
By Lawrence Kushner and Nehemia Polen
Reflects on the joy, gratitude, mystery and awe embedded in traditional prayers and blessings, and shows how you can imbue these familiar sacred words with your own sense of holiness. 5½ x 8¼, 176 pp, Hardcover, ISBN 1-58023-216-7 **$21.99**

The Book of Letters: A Mystical Hebrew Alphabet
Popular Hardcover Edition, 6 x 9, 80 pp, 2-color text, ISBN 1-879045-00-1 **$24.95**
Collector's Limited Edition, 9 x 12, 80 pp, gold foil embossed pages, w/limited edition silkscreened print, ISBN 1-879045-04-4 **$349.00**

The Book of Miracles: A Young Person's Guide to Jewish Spiritual Awareness
6 x 9, 96 pp, 2-color illus., Hardcover, ISBN 1-879045-78-8 **$16.95** *For ages 9–13*

The Book of Words: Talking Spiritual Life, Living Spiritual Talk
6 x 9, 160 pp, Quality PB, ISBN 1-58023-020-2 **$16.95**

Eyes Remade for Wonder: A Lawrence Kushner Reader *Introduction by Thomas Moore*
6 x 9, 240 pp, Quality PB, ISBN 1-58023-042-3 **$18.95;** Hardcover, ISBN 1-58023-014-8 **$23.95**

God Was in This Place & I, i Did Not Know
Finding Self, Spirituality and Ultimate Meaning 6 x 9, 192 pp, Quality PB, ISBN 1-879045-33-8 **$16.95**

Honey from the Rock: An Introduction to Jewish Mysticism
6 x 9, 176 pp, Quality PB, ISBN 1-58023-073-3 **$16.95**

Invisible Lines of Connection: Sacred Stories of the Ordinary
5½ x 8¼, 160 pp, Quality PB, ISBN 1-879045-98-2 **$15.95**

Jewish Spirituality—A Brief Introduction for Christians
5½ x 8¼, 112 pp, Quality PB Original, ISBN 1-58023-150-0 **$12.95**

The River of Light: Jewish Mystical Awareness 6 x 9, 192 pp, Quality PB, ISBN 1-58023-096-2 **$16.95**

The Way Into Jewish Mystical Tradition
6 x 9, 224 pp, Quality PB, ISBN 1-58023-200-0 **$18.99;** Hardcover, ISBN 1-58023-029-6 **$21.95**

Spirituality/Prayer

Pray Tell: A Hadassah Guide to Jewish Prayer
By Rabbi Jules Harlow, with contributions from Tamara Cohen, Rochelle Furstenberg, Rabbi Daniel Gordis, Leora Tanenbaum, and many others
Enriched with insight and wisdom from a broad variety of viewpoints.
8½ x 11, 400 pp, Quality PB, ISBN 1-58023-163-2 **$29.95**

My People's Prayer Book Series
Traditional Prayers, Modern Commentaries *Edited by Rabbi Lawrence A. Hoffman*
Provides diverse and exciting commentary to the traditional liturgy, helping modern men and women find new wisdom in Jewish prayer, and bring liturgy into their lives. Each book includes Hebrew text, modern translation, and commentaries from all perspectives of the Jewish world.

Vol. 1—The *Sh'ma* and Its Blessings
7 x 10, 168 pp, Hardcover, ISBN 1-879045-79-6 **$24.99**
Vol. 2—The *Amidah*
7 x 10, 240 pp, Hardcover, ISBN 1-879045-80-X **$24.95**
Vol. 3—*P'sukei D'zimrah* (Morning Psalms)
7 x 10, 240 pp, Hardcover, ISBN 1-879045-81-8 **$24.95**
Vol. 4—*Seder K'riat Hatorah* (The Torah Service)
7 x 10, 264 pp, Hardcover, ISBN 1-879045-82-6 **$23.95**
Vol. 5—*Birkhot Hashachar* (Morning Blessings)
7 x 10, 240 pp, Hardcover, ISBN 1-879045-83-4 **$24.95**
Vol. 6—*Tachanun* and Concluding Prayers
7 x 10, 240 pp, Hardcover, ISBN 1-879045-84-2 **$24.95**
Vol. 7—Shabbat at Home
7 x 10, 240 pp, Hardcover, ISBN 1-879045-85-0 **$24.95**
Vol. 8—*Kabbalat Shabbat* (Welcoming Shabbat in the Synagogue)
7 x 10, 240 pp, Hardcover, ISBN 1-58023-121-7 **$24.99**
Vol. 9—Welcoming the Night: *Minchah* and *Ma'ariv* (Afternoon and Evening Prayer) 7 x 10, 272 pp, Hardcover, ISBN 1-58023-262-0 **$24.99**

Spirituality/The Way Into... Series

The Way Into... Series offers an accessible and highly usable "guided tour" of the Jewish faith, people, history and beliefs—in total, an introduction to Judaism that will enable you to understand and interact with the sacred texts of the Jewish tradition. Each volume is written by a leading contemporary scholar and teacher, and explores one key aspect of Judaism. The Way Into... enables all readers to achieve a real sense of Jewish cultural literacy through guided study.

The Way Into Encountering God in Judaism *By Neil Gillman*
6 x 9, 240 pp, Quality PB, ISBN 1-58023-199-3 **$18.99**; Hardcover, ISBN 1-58023-025-3 **$21.95**

Also Available: **The Jewish Approach to God: A Brief Introduction for Christians**
By Neil Gillman 5½ x 8½, 192 pp, Quality PB, ISBN 1-58023-190-X **$16.95**

The Way Into Jewish Mystical Tradition *By Lawrence Kushner*
6 x 9, 224 pp, Quality PB, ISBN 1-58023-200-0 **$18.99**; Hardcover, ISBN 1-58023-029-6 **$21.95**

The Way Into Jewish Prayer *By Lawrence A. Hoffman*
6 x 9, 224 pp, Quality PB, ISBN 1-58023-201-9 **$18.99**; Hardcover, ISBN 1-58023-027-X **$21.95**

The Way Into the Relationship between Jews and Non-Jews: Searching for Boundaries and Bridges *By Michael A. Signer, PhD*
6 x 9, 225 pp (est.), Hardcover, ISBN 1-58023-267-1 **$24.99**

The Way Into Judaism and the Environment *By Jeremy Benstein, PhD*
6 x 9, 225 pp (est.), Hardcover, ISBN 1-58023-268-X **$24.99**

The Way Into *Tikkun Olam* **(Repairing the World)** *By Elliot N. Dorff*
6 x 9, 320 pp, Hardcover, ISBN 1-58023-269-8 **$24.99**

The Way Into Torah *By Norman J. Cohen*
6 x 9, 176 pp, Quality PB, ISBN 1-58023-198-5 **$16.99**; Hardcover, ISBN 1-58023-028-8 **$21.95**

Spirituality and Wellness

Aleph-Bet Yoga
Embodying the Hebrew Letters for Physical and Spiritual Well-Being
By Steven A. Rapp. Foreword by Tamar Frankiel, Ph.D., and Judy Greenfeld. Preface by Hart Lazer
7 x 10, 128 pp, b/w photos, Quality PB, Layflat binding, ISBN 1-58023-162-4 **$16.95**

Entering the Temple of Dreams
Jewish Prayers, Movements, and Meditations for the End of the Day
By Tamar Frankiel, Ph.D., and Judy Greenfeld
7 x 10, 192 pp, illus., Quality PB, ISBN 1-58023-079-2 **$16.95**

Jewish Paths toward Healing and Wholeness: A Personal Guide to Dealing with Suffering *By Rabbi Kerry M. Olitzky. Foreword by Debbie Friedman.*
6 x 9, 192 pp, Quality PB, ISBN 1-58023-068-7 **$15.95**

Minding the Temple of the Soul
Balancing Body, Mind, and Spirit through Traditional Jewish Prayer, Movement, and Meditation *By Tamar Frankiel, Ph.D., and Judy Greenfeld*
7 x 10, 184 pp, illus., Quality PB, ISBN 1-879045-64-8 **$16.95**
Audiotape of the Blessings and Meditations: 60 min. **$9.95**
Videotape of the Movements and Meditations: 46 min. **$20.00**

Theology/Philosophy

Aspects of Rabbinic Theology
By Solomon Schechter. New Introduction by Dr. Neil Gillman.
6 x 9, 448 pp, Quality PB, ISBN 1-879045-24-9 **$19.95**

Broken Tablets: Restoring the Ten Commandments and Ourselves
Edited by Rachel S. Mikva. Introduction by Lawrence Kushner. Afterword by Arnold Jacob Wolf.
6 x 9, 192 pp, Quality PB, ISBN 1-58023-158-6 **$16.95**; Hardcover, ISBN 1-58023-066-0 **$21.95**

Creating an Ethical Jewish Life
A Practical Introduction to Classic Teachings on How to Be a Jew
By Dr. Byron L. Sherwin and Seymour J. Cohen
6 x 9, 336 pp, Quality PB, ISBN 1-58023-114-4 **$19.95**

The Death of Death: Resurrection and Immortality in Jewish Thought
By Dr. Neil Gillman 6 x 9, 336 pp, Quality PB, ISBN 1-58023-081-4 **$18.95**

Evolving Halakhah: A Progressive Approach to Traditional Jewish Law
By Rabbi Dr. Moshe Zemer
6 x 9, 480 pp, Quality PB, ISBN 1-58023-127-6 **$29.95**; Hardcover, ISBN 1-58023-002-4 **$40.00**

Hasidic Tales: Annotated & Explained
By Rabbi Rami Shapiro. Foreword by Andrew Harvey, SkyLight Illuminations series editor.
5½ x 8½, 240 pp, Quality PB, ISBN 1-893361-86-1 **$16.95** *(A SkyLight Paths Book)*

A Heart of Many Rooms: Celebrating the Many Voices within Judaism
By Dr. David Hartman 6 x 9, 352 pp, Quality PB, ISBN 1-58023-156-X **$19.95**

The Hebrew Prophets: Selections Annotated & Explained
Translation & Annotation by Rabbi Rami Shapiro. Foreword by Zalman M. Schachter-Shalomi
5½ x 8½, 224 pp, Quality PB, ISBN 1-59473-037-7 **$16.99** *(A SkyLight Paths book)*

Keeping Faith with the Psalms: Deepen Your Relationship with God Using the
Book of Psalms *By Daniel F. Polish* 6 x 9, 320 pp, Quality PB, ISBN 1-58023-300-7 **$18.99**;
Hardcover, ISBN 1-58023-179-9 **$24.95**

The Last Trial
On the Legends and Lore of the Command to Abraham to Offer Isaac as a Sacrifice
By Shalom Spiegel. New Introduction by Judah Goldin.
6 x 9, 208 pp, Quality PB, ISBN 1-879045-29-X **$18.95**

A Living Covenant: The Innovative Spirit in Traditional Judaism
By Dr. David Hartman 6 x 9, 368 pp, Quality PB, ISBN 1-58023-011-3 **$18.95**

Love and Terror in the God Encounter
The Theological Legacy of Rabbi Joseph B. Soloveitchik
By Dr. David Hartman
6 x 9, 240 pp, Quality PB, ISBN 1-58023-176-4 **$19.95**; Hardcover, ISBN 1-58023-112-8 **$25.00**

The Personhood of God: Biblical Theology, Human Faith and the Divine Image
By Dr. Yochanan Muffs; Foreword by Dr. David Hartman
6 x 9, 240 pp, Hardcover, ISBN 1-58023-265-5 **$24.99**

The Spirit of Renewal: Finding Faith after the Holocaust
By Rabbi Edward Feld 6 x 9, 224 pp, Quality PB, ISBN 1-879045-40-0 **$16.95**

Tormented Master: The Life and Spiritual Quest of Rabbi Nahman of Bratslav
By Dr. Arthur Green 6 x 9, 416 pp, Quality PB, ISBN 1-879045-11-7 **$19.99**

Your Word Is Fire: The Hasidic Masters on Contemplative Prayer
Edited and translated by Dr. Arthur Green and Barry W. Holtz
6 x 9, 160 pp, Quality PB, ISBN 1-879045-25-7 **$15.95**

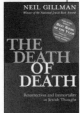

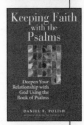
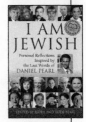

I Am Jewish
Personal Reflections Inspired by the Last Words of Daniel Pearl
Almost 150 Jews—both famous and not—from all walks of life, from all around
the world, write about Identity, Heritage, Covenant / Chosenness and Faith,
Humanity and Ethnicity, and *Tikkun Olam* and Justice.
Edited by Judea and Ruth Pearl
6 x 9, 304 pp, Deluxe PB w/flaps, ISBN 1-58023-259-0 **$18.99**; Hardcover, ISBN 1-58023-183-7 **$24.99**
Download a free copy of the *I Am Jewish Teacher's Guide* at our website:
www.jewishlights.com

About Jewish Lights

People of all faiths and backgrounds yearn for books that attract, engage, educate, and spiritually inspire.

Our principal goal is to stimulate thought and help all people learn about who the Jewish People are, where they come from, and what the future can be made to hold. While people of our diverse Jewish heritage are the primary audience, our books speak to people in the Christian world as well and will broaden their understanding of Judaism and the roots of their own faith.

We bring to you authors who are at the forefront of spiritual thought and experience. While each has something different to say, they all say it in a voice that you can hear.

Our books are designed to welcome you and then to engage, stimulate, and inspire. We judge our success not only by whether or not our books are beautiful and commercially successful, but by whether or not they make a difference in your life.

For your information and convenience, at the back of this book we have provided a list of other Jewish Lights books you might find interesting and useful. They cover all the categories of your life:

Bar/Bat Mitzvah	Life Cycle
Bible Study / Midrash	Meditation
Children's Books	Parenting
Congregation Resources	Prayer
Current Events / History	Ritual / Sacred Practice
Ecology	Spirituality
Fiction: Mystery, Science Fiction	Theology / Philosophy
Grief / Healing	Travel
Holidays / Holy Days	Twelve Steps
Inspiration	Women's Interest
Kabbalah / Mysticism / Enneagram	

Stuart M. Matlins, Publisher

Or phone, fax, mail or e-mail to: **JEWISH LIGHTS Publishing**
Sunset Farm Offices, Route 4 • P.O. Box 237 • Woodstock, Vermont 05091
Tel: (802) 457-4000 • Fax: (802) 457-4004 • www.jewishlights.com
Credit card orders: (800) 962-4544 (8:30AM–5:30PM ET Monday–Friday)
Generous discounts on quantity orders. SATISFACTION GUARANTEED. Prices subject to change.